CREATING SUCCESS IN THE CLASSROOM!

CREATING SUCCESS IN THE CLASSROOM!

Visual Organizers and How to Use Them

Patti Tarquin

and

Sharon Walker

1997
TEACHER IDEAS PRESS
A Division of
Libraries Unlimited, Inc.
Englewood, Colorado

*To our families
and the teachers
throughout New York state
who opened their classrooms to us . . .*

TEACHER IDEAS PRESS
A Division of
Libraries Unlimited, Inc.
P.O. Box 6633
Englewood, CO 80155-6633
1-800-237-6124

Production Editor: Kevin W. Perizzolo
Copy Editor: Jason Cook
Proofreader: Susie Sigman
Design and Layout: Pamela J. Getchell

Library of Congress Cataloging-in-Publication Data

Tarquin, Patti, 1946-
    Creating success in the classroom! : visual organizers and how to use them / Patti Tarquin and Sharon Walker.
    xiii, 235 p. 22x28 cm.
    Includes bibliographical references.
    ISBN 1-56308-437-6
    1. Visual learning. 2. Audio-visual aids. 3. Thought and thinking--Study and teaching.   I. Walker, Sharon, 1946-   .
II. Title.
LB1067.5.T37   1996
    371.3'35--dc20
                                                    96-28098
                                                        CIP

CONTENTS

Preface xi

1 Story Maps 1
   What Are They? 1
   Why Use Them? 1
   How to Use Them 1
      Whole-Group 2
      Small-Group 2
      Individual 2
      Pre-Reading 2
   Suggestions for Use 3
      Primary Format 3
      Intermediate Format 5
      The Story Map As a Pre-Reading Strategy 6
      Chapter-Book Format 6
      The #!#! TV 7
      Nonfiction Format 7
      Math Format 9
      The Writing Classroom 11
      Sharing Story Maps 12
      Narrative Format 12
   Assessment Opportunities 14

2 Venn Diagrams 24
   What Are They? 24
   Why Use Them? 24
   How to Use Them 24
      Whole-Group 25
      Small-Group 25
      Individual 25
   Suggestions for Use 25
      The Reading Classroom 25
      The Language Arts Classroom 26
      The #!#! TV 27
      The Mathematics Classroom 28
      The Science Classroom 32
      The Social Studies Classroom 32
      The Music Classroom 32
      The Physical Education Classroom 33
      The Art Classroom 33
   Assessment Opportunities 33

3 Frameworks for Webbing 37
   What Are They? 37
   Why Use Them? 37
   How to Use Them 37
      Whole-Group 38
      Small-Group 38
      Individual 38
   Suggestions for Use 39
      Traditional Format 39
      Outlining 42
      Vocabulary 43
      Teacher Lesson Plans 44
      Discussion Webs 45
      The #!#! TV 47
      Tree Format 48
      The Mathematics Classroom 48
      The Reading Classroom 50
      The Writing Classroom 51
   Assessment Opportunities 51

4 The KWL Frameworks 58
   What Are They? 58
   Why Use Them? 58
   How to Use Them 58
      Whole-Group 59
      Small-Group 59
      Individual 59
   Suggestions for Use 59
      Switch the Last Two Columns 60
      Eliminate the Middle 61
      Eliminate the First Column 62
      Change the Letters 64
      Another Letter Change 67
   Assessment Opportunities 67

5 Main Idea/Supporting Details: Frameworks 71
   What Are They? 71
   Why Use Them? 71
   How to Use Them 72
      Whole-Group 72
      Small-Group 73
      Individual 73
   Suggestions for Use 73
      Main Idea/Supporting Details Format 73
      Music/Art Connection 77
      Main Idea/Supporting Details Topic Format 78
      Notetaking Form 81
      Two Subject: Main Idea/Supporting Details 82

The Writing Classroom 84
The #!#! TV 85
Assessment Opportunities 86

6 Cause-and-Effect Frameworks 94
What Are They? 94
Why Use Them? 94
How to Use Them 95
Whole-Group 95
Small-Group 95
Individual 95
Suggestions for Use 96
Effect-and-Cause Format 96
The Science Classroom 97
Social Behavior 98
The Mathematics Classroom 99
Cause-and-Effect Chains 100
The Science Classroom Revisited 101
The Mathematics Classroom Revisited 103
The #!#! TV 103
One Cause/Many Effects Format 104
Many Causes/One Effect Format 105
The Writing Classroom 106
Assessment Opportunities 108

7 Classification Frameworks 116
What Are They? 116
Why Use Them? 116
How to Use Them 116
Whole-Group 117
Small-Group 117
Individual 117
Suggestions for Use 117
Classification Boxes 118
The Science Classroom 119
The Reading Classroom 121
The Social Studies Classroom 122
The Language Classroom 123
Notetaking 123
Parts of Speech Classifier 124
In a Class by Itself 126
The #!#! TV 128
Assessment Opportunities 129

8 Fact/Opinion Frameworks 138
 What Are They? 138
 Why Use Them? 138
 How to Use Them 138
  Whole-Group 139
  Small-Group 139
  Individual 140
 Suggestions for Use 140
  Advertisements 141
  Editorials 143
  The Science Classroom 144
  The Speaking/Writing Classroom 146
 Assessment Opportunities 148

9 Circle Frameworks 156
 What Are They? 156
 Why Use Them? 156
 How to Use Them 157
  Whole-Group 157
  Small-Group 157
  Individual 158
 Suggestions for Use 158
  Vocabulary Development 158
  Word Analysis 159
  Parts of Speech 160
  Comprehension 161
  Character Analysis 166
  The Writing Classroom 168
  The Math/Science Classroom 171
 Assessment Opportunities 172

10 Semantic Feature Analysis Frameworks 180
 What Are They? 180
 Why Use Them? 180
 How to Use Them 181
  Whole-Group 181
  Small-Group 182
  Individual 182
 Suggestions for Use 182
 Assessment Opportunities 188

11 Flowcharts 193
 What Are They? 193
 Why Use Them? 193
 How to Use Them 194
  Whole-Group 194
  Small-Group 194
  Individual 194

Suggestions for Use 195
  Giving Directions 195
  The Writing Classroom 196
  The Reading Classroom 198
  The Science Classroom 200
  The Social Studies Classroom 200
  The Physical Education Classroom 201
Assessment Opportunities 203

12 Charts 207
What Are They? 207
Why Use Them? 207
How to Use Them 208
  Whole-Group 208
  Small-Group 208
  Individual 208
Suggestions for Use 209
  Vocabulary Development 209
  Before, During, and After Reading 212
Assessment Opportunities 223

Final Thoughts 229

References 233

About the Authors 235

Preface

What Are Visual Organizers?

Visual Organizers are called many things, including graphic organizers, formal organizers, and visual strategies. They are visual representations of concepts and ideas. When used in classrooms, they provide students with tools to make thought and organization processes visible. They serve as organizational frameworks to promote thinking and language development.

Why Use Visual Organizers?

Teachers use frameworks as a cognitive strategy to visually demonstrate to students how ideas and information in a specific problem, passage, text, or unit of study are related and organized. When a framework is completed, the student can visualize how major ideas are related

to their own prior knowledge,

to subordinate ideas, and

to other facts and ideas from other sources.

The use of frameworks provides a stimulating way to cover particular topics of interest in greater depth. Because the frameworks require specific information, teachers challenge students to search out ideas from their course of study or tap into their prior knowledge and relate their ideas in a conceptual, organized way. The strategies particularly assist students with restructuring ideas and processing information.

The National Council of Teachers of Mathematics, in Standard 2 of the NCTM Standards notes that mathematics is a form of communication. The Council encourages the use of organized thinking so that students can reflect on mathematics and clarify their thinking about it. Further encouragement is given to discussing, reading, writing, listening, and viewing mathematics in a logical manner. Frameworks become a means to an end in helping the teacher meet the suggestions of this Standard. Frameworks also help the student develop logical conclusions about mathematics, as recommended in Standard 3. By developing relationships within a framework, the student sees that math makes sense.

Project 2061, Science for All Americans emphasizes ideas and thinking skills in science. No longer are students expected to memorize a special vocabulary or procedures but instead are encouraged to use details to enhance their general understanding. By recommending an emphasis on teaching fewer topics more thoroughly, the door has been opened to using frameworks, which organize a student's thought processes and allows subsequent investigation of a topic. Frameworks also lend themselves to research beyond the textbook, fulfilling another recommendation of *Project 2061*.

ASSESSMENT OPPORTUNITIES

Classroom assessment increases student participation and involvement. As teachers use blank frameworks for assessment purposes, they will reinforce metacognition (learner's awareness, understanding, and control of his/her learning process) by

teaching students how to use the framework,

providing guided practice in using the framework,

encouraging students to share their responses with one another, and

giving students feedback regarding their responses.

Empty frameworks can help students better organize and reorganize their memories of the material they are learning. Frameworks prompt students to consider how their own ideas and concepts are related, providing a powerful tool for self-assessment and teacher assessment.

Once a student has completed a framework, teachers have a valuable tool for assessing

how well students organize their own thinking,

how accurately students can construct meaning based on their prior knowledge,

how accurately students can restructure and record ideas from material, and

how effectively students can put major concepts from an organizer into their own writing or speaking.

While students are working on frameworks individually, in partners or small groups, it is important to take anecdotal notes that indicate

the ease with which students use the frameworks,

how they use the frameworks (which part they filled in first), and

the creativity of the responses.

Twelve frameworks will be introduced. Each chapter begins with a discussion of the framework(s) under the headings "What Are They?," "Why Use Them?," and "How to Use Them." "Suggestions for Use" includes practical tips and examples from several curriculum areas. Classroom assessment techniques are discussed in each chapter under "Assessment Opportunities." Holistic rubrics, checklists, assessment tasks, and grading outlines are provided as examples. If applicable, suggestions are made for writing and speaking assessments. Research has demonstrated that, for assessment to be effective, the goal in any classroom should be to involve students in designing the assessment tool. If involved, students will have a clear picture of the assessment task and how it will be evaluated. Assessment results should be shared with students. Students should be allowed to assess the assessment. It is through this teacher-student feedback that assessment tools become refined.

We feel that the frameworks included here can be used by students of all ages. We have used them with students in kindergarten through 12th grade. It is our hope that you will find this book to be a practical and valuable resource, with suggestions for activities that do not require weeks of preparation. Enjoy!

ONE

Story Maps

What Are They?

Story maps are vertical flow maps. They help students understand that stories have well-formed components: setting, characters, problem/goal, action (steps taken to resolve the problem or reach the goal), and a solution or end.

Why Use Them?

- Students can improve their comprehension when they read or listen to a selection by organizing the information into some kind of clear visual framework.

- When used as a pre-reading strategy, students can form a mental picture and build anticipation of what is to be read or listened to.

- Once completed, students can write effective summaries from their maps or retell the story orally using the map as a guide.

How to Use Them

Teacher models and guides:

1. Point out that stories have well-formed components.

2. Explain to students that questions about a story will help them remember and understand the story. A story map will also help them see how parts of a story fit together.

3. Read a story to students.

4. Ask students to recall specific information and complete a story map together.

5. Reread the story and check to see if the key elements listed are correct.

6. Once the story map has been completed, demonstrate to students how a story can be restructured—simply by referring to the story map.

Whole-Group

The teacher or a student acts as a scribe and records information from a story the class has read or listened to on an appropriate class story map. It is a good idea to have the class story map enlarged and laminated. This group mapping can be completed during or after reading.

Small-Group

After the class has read or listened to a story, cut up the large class or individual story map into its component parts. Give each group a part: one group has characters, another action, and so on. After a certain time period, have the small groups come together and assemble a class story map. Or, have each group complete an entire story map and then compare it to the maps from other groups. Students in "literature circles" could complete story maps of their book and share it with the entire class.

Individual

Each student reads a story and independently fills out an appropriate story map.

Pre-Reading

The teacher supplies the title, words, and phrases from the selection. Have students place the words and phrases in the section of the story map they think is most appropriate. After reading, return to the story map and confirm or make changes. This activity can be done with the whole group, in small groups, or individually.

Suggestions for Use

Primary Format

This format lends itself to the introduction of distinct parts of the story. Students can fold a paper into thirds and draw a picture for the beginning, middle, and the end. When working with young children, turn the paper horizontally to allow reinforcement of left to right progression. It is often easier to have younger children first draw the beginning, then the end, and finish with the middle.

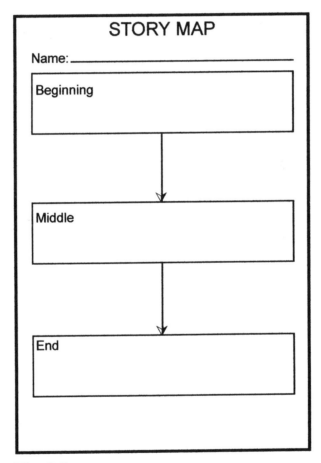

Fig. 1.1.

Students should be encouraged to label each picture with a word or sentence. When the story map is completed, encourage students to retell the story to a partner, small group, or the teacher, using the story map as a guide.

Once students are comfortable with the beginning primary format, the boxes can be relabeled. Have students draw or list characters, setting, problem/goal in the appropriate boxes. Once students are comfortable with these categories,

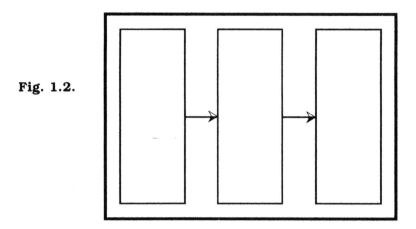

Fig. 1.2.

add a fourth category: solution/outcome. This is an excellent map to use in the jigsaw manner—have four students read the same book and have each one fill out one of the categories. Students share their assigned box with the group. Once the group has agreed, the story map can be pasted together. The use of logos (see figure 1.3) helps remind students what part of the story map they are working on.

Figure 1.3 is a map completed in a jigsaw manner by a first-grade class.

Title: *Where the Wild Things Are*
Author: Maurice Sendak

Character (s)	Max Mom Wild Things
Setting	Max's Room Land of the Wild Things
Problem/Goal	Max was sent to bed without his supper
Solution/End	Max sailed back to his room and his supper was waiting for him

Fig. 1.3.

INTERMEDIATE FORMAT

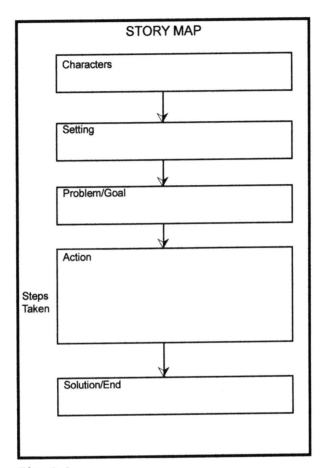

Fig. 1.4.

This format introduces students to the elements of a story. To facilitate the process, ask the following questions:

Characters   Who was involved in the story?

Setting   Where and when did the events in the story take place?

Problem/Goal   What started the chain of events in the story?

Action   What events took place to reach the solution/end?

Solution/End   What happened as a result of the main character's actions? How was the problem solved or the goal reached?

Once the story map has been completed, encourage students to summarize the story either orally or in writing, using the map as a guide.

The Story Map As a Pre-Reading Strategy

Give the students the title, author, and a list of words and phrases (sentences for a primary map) from a story they have not read. Have them place these words and phrases in the section of the story map they think is appropriate. Read the story to students or have them read it independently or in pairs. After reading, return to the pre-reading map and confirm predictions. This is particularly helpful if you think a story may be difficult for students to comprehend or if it contains difficult vocabulary.

Example—*The Stranger* by Chris Van Allsburg

Mr. Bailey hit the stranger with his car   a stranger   the rabbits weren't afraid
the leaves on the trees turned colors   the stranger left   Mrs. Bailey
the stranger didn't talk   Katy   the stranger never tired
Mr. Bailey   the leaves on the trees didn't change colors

Chapter-Book Format

Story maps can "grow" as students read a chapter book. Have students fill out character and setting boxes as they discover this information in the text. Once the problem/goal has been established, students should complete that box. As each chapter is read, have students write a brief summary under the action block. At the end of the book, students should establish the outcome. This provides students with a vertical flow chart—an excellent information sheet for them to use when writing a book report.

The hardest part of the chapter-book format is getting students to summarize a chapter in one or two sentences. Remind them to concentrate on the key events or overall feel of the chapter. It is best to introduce this format with a chapter book the teacher is reading to the class. Guide students in writing summary statements by asking:

What significant things happened to the main character?

What happened in this chapter to set the scene for the next chapter?

Figure 1.5 is an example of a chapter-book story map.

Title: Whalesong	Author: Robert Siegel

Characters:	Hruna, Lewte, Great Whale - Hralenkana
Setting:	Ocean

Problem/Goal:	Hruna must grow up and learn the way of the whales.
Action:	Hruna plays with Lewte and learns about the ways of the whales. Hruna is grazed by a harpoon and is threatened by a typhoon. Hruna leaves Lewte and his parents to go on the Lonely Cruise. Hruna meets Hralenkana - the Great Whale. Hruna finds Lewte in a lagoon with the captured dolphins and rescues her. Hruna and Lewte mate and return to their pod. The pod runs into human hunters while looking for food. Hruna insists on facing the hunters alone but the Great Whale appears and sacrifices himself to save them all.
Solution/End:	Hruna learned the ways of the whales. Hruna grows up and is the new leader of the pod.

Fig. 1.5.

The #!#! TV

We live with the reality of children watching television. Many children do not realize their favorite sitcom is a written story. Ask students to complete a story map of a specific television show or a show of their choice as a homework assignment. They can share it with the class orally or by placing it on a bulletin board. As a follow-up writing assignment, ask students to fill out a story map for a future show. If time permits and students are interested, they can write a story or play from their map.

Nonfiction Format

Changing headings allows students to map out nonfiction selections. A biography or an article pertaining to a certain topic (e.g., endangered species) can be mapped and provide students with an opportunity to organize the information into a visual framework.

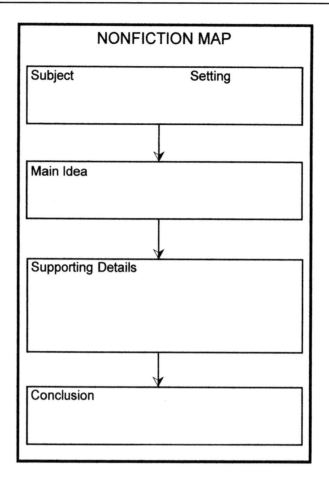

Fig. 1.6.

Figure 1.7 is a nonfiction map for Beethoven that was completed in a music class.

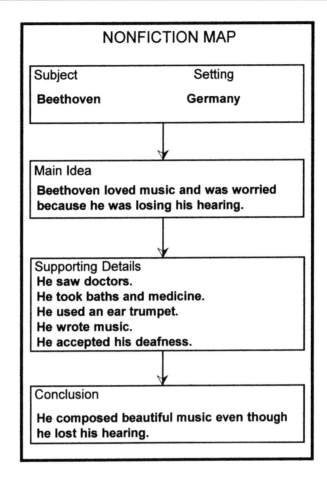

Fig. 1.7.

This map lends itself to describing a famous person in history, art, or music; a scientific event (e.g., development of space travel); or an historical occurrence (e.g., War of 1812). Story mapping should not be limited to literature.

Math Format

Any word problem can be mapped. This process gives students a clear visual of the important parts of the word problem and an area to show the steps they took in solving the problem. Occasionally, have students write, in their own words, how they solved the problem (in the section "Steps to Solve Problem"). This will provide the teacher with a clear picture of the thought process the student goes through when problem-solving.

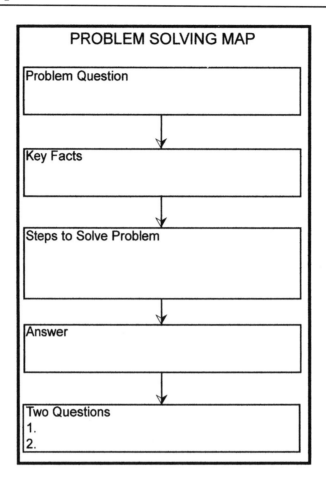

Fig. 1.8.

An example of a two-step problem:

Maria has 80 cents. It costs 30 cents for one candy bar.

She buys two candy bars. Can she buy another one?

The two questions for the final box should be posted in the classroom:

1. What does this answer mean?

2. Does this answer make sense?

Figure 1.9 is a sample story map for math.

PROBLEM SOLVING MAP

Problem Question

   Can Maria buy another candy bar?

Key Facts

   Has 80 cents. Bought two candy bars for 30 cents each.

Steps to Solve Problem

   I multiplied 30 X 2. Then I knew Maria spent 60 cents to buy two candy bars.
   Then I subtracted 60 cents from 80 cents to see how much money Maria had
   left.

Answer

   No, Maria could not buy another candy bar.

Two Questions

1.   Maria doesn't have enough money for another candy bar.
2.   Yes.

Fig. 1.9.

The Writing Classroom

Story maps are especially successful in the writing classroom. Students can complete a story map after writing a story of their own. This serves as an excellent self-assessment tool to indicate to the student important elements overlooked. It also can be used in the pre-writing stage to help students visualize the story and get a sense of story line. Students as young as first grade can be introduced to the primary map as an effective tool for planning their story. This often eliminates having a story with no end or middle.

A story map can serve as an excellent springboard for writing a newspaper article:

Problem/Goal:	Headline
Setting:	Dateline
Solution/End:	Introductory statement
Actions:	Body of the article (from the most important to the least)

The order in a newspaper article is different from that of a normal story due to the possibility that an editor will have less space than was originally assigned to the story. The journalist knows that if the story is run, at least the first paragraph will appear, so the article must begin with the conclusion. The body of the article will require that students write their actions from the most important to the least important for the same reason. The story map will allow them to brainstorm importance before they start to write.

SHARING STORY MAPS

Students, after completing a story map, can share it with a partner, another class, the librarian, principal, and so on. The person(s) receiving the story map will retell the story using the map. The student can then ask questions that are not directly answered on the map and then read the story to the person(s). This activity works very well with an older student visiting a younger class, i.e.: person retells the story of *Whalesong* using the Chapter Book story map. The student may ask the following questions:

"What do you think the Lonely Cruise is?" (record answers)

"Hruna finds Lewte in a lagoon with captured dolphins. Who do you think captured them, how did they capture them and why?" (record)

" Why did the Great Whale sacrifice his life for the other whales?" (record)

This will have to be modeled with students at first but it is an activity that will encourage higher level thinking skills and help build anticipation for the listener. This is an activity the teacher can use with the whole group when introducing a new read-aloud to the class.

NARRATIVE FORMAT

The narrative story map usually contains the following components:

Character(s)	The main people in the story
Setting	The context in which the story takes place: time, location
Initiating Event	The event that starts the chain of events
Reaction	How the main characters react to the initiating event
Goal	What the main characters decide to do—what goal is set
Consequence	What did the main characters do to meet their goal
Resolution	How did the goal turn out

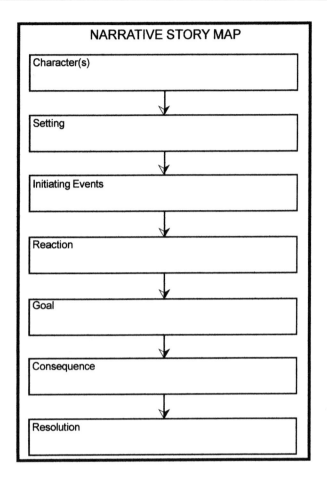

Fig. 1.10.

Guide students through this map at first by using the following questions:

The main character(s) were _____

The story took place _____

What was the event that really got everything going?

How did the main characters react to this event?

The main characters decided to take action. What was their goal?

What steps did the main characters have to take in order to meet their goal?

Did they meet their goal?

This is an excellent pre-writing strategy for students to plan their own narrative. Have students complete the story map based on a movie or television program they watch.

ASSESSMENT OPPORTUNITIES

Have students use completed story maps to write a summary or orally retell a story. Note what key elements are included/left out. Ask, how has the student:

organized the story?

structured information from the story?

successfully demonstrated comprehension of the story?

The story map provides an excellent tool for evaluating listening skills. Read a story to students. As you reread the story have them complete a story map. Do children lose details while they're listening? Do they zero in on problem and solution and miss key events in between? The teacher can readily identify where listening skills are breaking down.

Completing a story map accurately reflects comprehension of a story. If a student successfully completes the map, solid comprehension is indicated. When a student completes a map with significant omissions, it serves as a tool for teachers to detect what elements a student is missing when silently reading a selection. Perhaps a student can effectively recall the beginning and end of a story but not the middle. This may indicate that a student rushes through or stops thinking about what is being read during reading. Another student may effectively demonstrate the recall of events in a story but cannot determine the problem/goal correctly. This may indicate the student has a difficult time "getting" the big picture.

In the math format, a successfully completed map will indicate that a student can clearly identify the parts of a problem and follows the necessary steps to solve it. Requiring this during testing, will not only furnish the teacher valuable information, but will force the student to go through these steps.

Teachers need to observe children while they complete a story map:

What parts do they fill in first?

Do they need to return to the story for details?

Does filling in one part jog a memory of another part?

Do they fill in parts accurately?

When writing their own stories can they use a map to:

identify story components in their own writing

use a map to help plan their writing

This observation of a student's completion and use of a story map can provide a valuable information source for the teacher.

When evaluating the story map, two forms can be used and kept in a portfolio: The Student Checklist (figure 1.11) and the Evaluation Checklist (figure 1.12). Students may place a checkmark or a yes or no in the boxes provided. A teacher can write a comment in the space or write yes or no.

Word of caution—some stories lend themselves to story mapping better than others—try it yourself before asking students to complete.

STUDENT CHECKLIST FOR STORY MAPPING	
I listed the key characters	
I identified the setting	
If there was more than one setting I included all settings	
I stated the problem	
I stated the goal	
I listed key events from the story in the action box	
The resolution shows how the problem was solved	
The end shows if the goal was reached or not	

Fig. 1.11.

EVALUATION CHECKLIST FOR STORY MAPPING	
Name:	
Identifies the key characters	
Defines setting	
Defines settings if there is more than one	
Identifies problem or goal	
Identifies problem and goal when both exist in story	
Effectively summarizes the events Events in the action box are listed clearly and succinctly	

Matches
   the resolution with the problem
   the outcome with the goal	

Comments	

Fig. 1.12.

STORY MAP

Name: _____

Beginning

Middle

End

STORY MAP

Author/Title : _____

Character(s)	
Setting	
Problem/Goal	
Solution/End	

STORY MAP

Characters

Setting

Problem/Goal

Steps
Taken

Action

Solution/End

From *Creating Success in the Classroom!* © 1996. Teacher Ideas Press. (800) 237-6124.

NONFICTION MAP

Subject   **Setting**

Main Idea

Supporting Details

Conclusion

PROBLEM SOLVING MAP

Problem Questions

Key Facts

Steps to Solve Problem

Answer

Two Questions
1.
2.

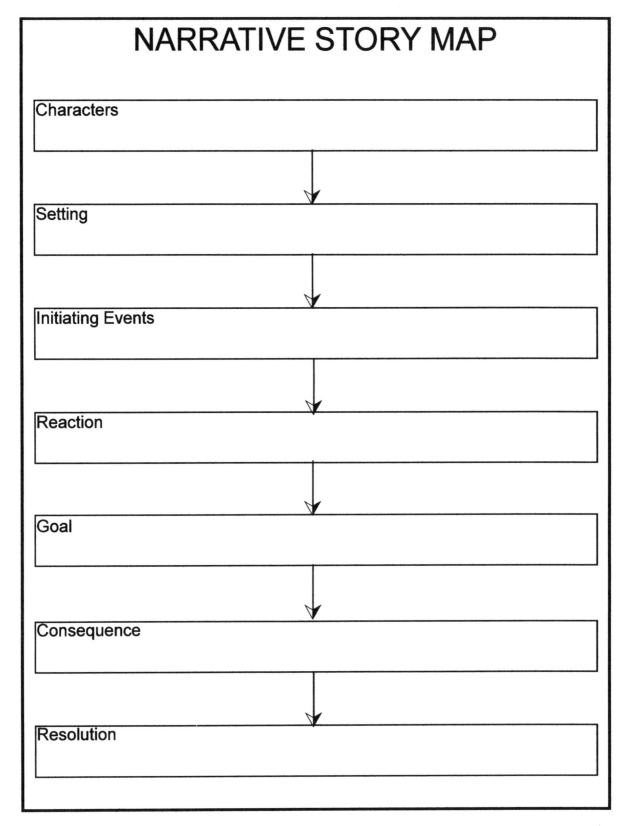

NARRATIVE STORY MAP

Characters

Setting

Initiating Events

Reaction

Goal

Consequence

Resolution

DUAL STORY MAP
Comparing Two Stories

Elements	Story A	Story B
Characters		
Setting		
Problem/Goal		
Solution/End		
Mood		

Using this story map, write a paragraph comparing the two stories you read.

TWO

Venn Diagrams

What Are They?

Named after John Venn (1832–1923)—the first person to use the diagrams in a general way in mathematics—a Venn diagram is a thinking strategy that helps analyze similarities and differences between two or more concepts. Traditionally used in mathematics, they can be used as a framework for constructing comparisons.

Why Use Them?

Students will

- become actively involved in defining attributes while viewing, listening, reading, or notetaking.

- visually focus on similarities and differences while reading, listening, viewing, or notetaking.

- actively restructure information into similarities and differences while reading, listening, viewing, or notetaking.

How to Use Them

Teacher models and guides:

1. Choose two characters or concepts to be compared. Home and school are two excellent topics to use as an introduction to the Venn diagram.

2 Brainstorm the attributes of two characters or concepts.

24

3. Reach a consensus as to where information will be recorded (in which circle part).

4. Record information.

Whole-Group

The teacher or a student acts as a scribe and records information from the class. The teacher chooses two characters or concepts to be compared. The class brainstorms the attributes of the two characters or concepts. The class reaches a consensus as to where the information will be recorded and so records it.

Small-Group

The teacher chooses two characters or concepts for each group to compare. They may be the same for all groups, or each group may have their own. The group brainstorms while the recorder writes down the information. The information is recorded in circle parts according to the group consensus. The groups come together and share information with the whole class. Discussion should be held about any differences in opinion.

Individual

The teacher chooses two characters or concepts for individuals to compare. The student identifies attributes and places them in desired positions. The student shares with the whole class, a partner, or hands it in for evaluation.

Suggestions for Use

The Venn diagram is compatible to all content areas.

The Reading Classroom

The Venn diagram can be used to show similarities and differences between characters within a story.

Figure 2.1 shows a comparison of Wilbur and Charlotte in *Charlotte's Web* by E. B. White.

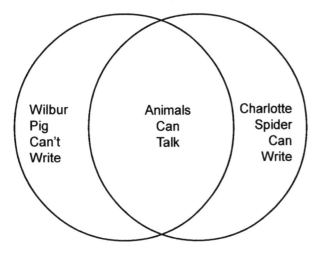

Fig. 2.1.

In this lesson, the objective was to find a corresponding difference and similarity to the first attribute mentioned about each animal. When one student mentions that Wilbur is a pig, the teacher can elicit the responses that Charlotte was a spider and that they were both animals. When it is mentioned that Charlotte can write, then it can be noted that Wilbur cannot but that they both can talk.

Stories, especially tall tales, fairy tales, and plays, often come in other versions. After students have read one version, a listening activity could involve the teacher reading another version of the story while the student fills in differences and similarities. This could also be a "center" activity. Two excellent books to start with are *The Seven Chinese Brothers* by Margaret Mahy and *The Five Chinese Brothers* by Claire Huchet Bishop and Kurt Wiese. Students will not only enjoy the stories but the similarities and differences are very obvious.

The Venn diagram can be used to compare characters, settings, or mood within a story or from two different stories. This is an excellent strategy for comparing two works from the same author, two newspapers or research articles reporting on the same subject, or a nonfiction article with a fictional piece (e.g., an article on the rain forest and *The Great Kapok Tree* by Lynne Cherry).

The Language Arts Classroom

Venn diagrams can be used to effectively teach a grammar lesson. They allow students to see how the parts of speech relate to each other (e.g., the comparison of adjectives and adverbs). When one concept has been introduced and it is time to introduce the other, students will be more confident if they know the similarities and differences. First write both definitions on the chalkboard, as in figure 2.2.

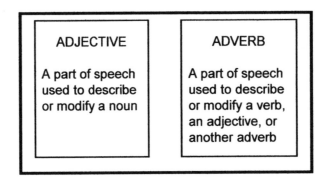

Fig. 2.2.

Next, add their similarities and differences to the Venn diagram, as in figure 2.3.

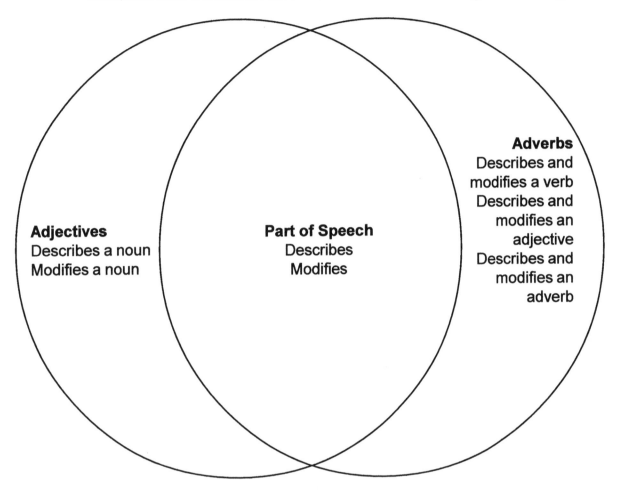

Fig. 2.3.

The Venn diagram can also be used to compare writing genres (e.g., narrative with descriptive piece), letters (e.g., business with friendly), and sentence structure (e.g., compound with simple). It provides students with a visual reminder of the differences that occur because of form. It is also an effective tool for a pre-writing activity. Whenever students are writing a comparison paper, they should always begin by placing their thoughts within this framework.

ThE #!#! TV

Assign a Venn diagram as a homework assignment to compare two television sitcoms, two characters on a favorite show, or two news reports of the same event (e.g., local coverage versus national).

THE MATHEMATICS CLASSROOM

Venn diagrams have traditionally been used in mathematics when discussing sets, especially in conjunction with union and intersection. Students often have difficulty when moving to the inverse of an operation that they have just learned (e.g., moving from addition to subtraction, or from multiplication to division). Their realization of a connection can be sharpened by the use of the Venn diagram (see figure 2.4).

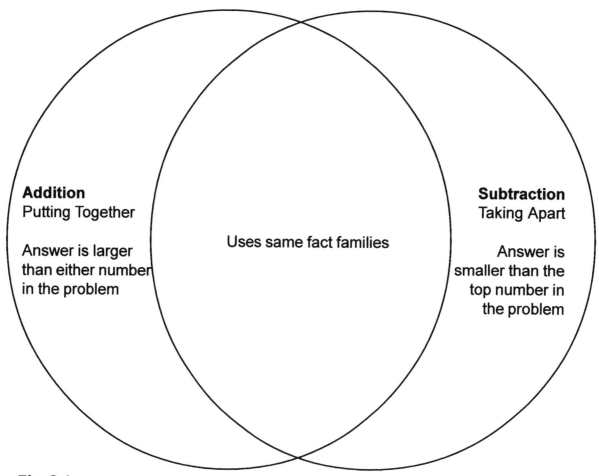

Addition
Putting Together

Answer is larger than either number in the problem

Uses same fact families

Subtraction
Taking Apart

Answer is smaller than the top number in the problem

Fig. 2.4.

An excellent way to introduce and quickly practice Venn diagrams is through the use of Attribute Blocks. Take one set and attach "peel-and-stick" magnets to the back of each. Draw a large Venn diagram on the chalkboard and then play a guessing game with students. Place pieces with one attribute in one part of the diagram and pieces with another attribute in the other. Have students guess the label for each circle. Afterwards, students place pieces with the shared attributes in the center. This activity can be done quickly throughout the year whenever there are a few spare moments. Start with the easy ones and move to the more difficult as the year progresses.

(CAUTION: When setting up Attribute Blocks, be sure that the only attribute they *all* share is the one you denoted by the label. For example, if you want the label to be "same color," make sure there are a variety of shapes, sizes, and thicknesses in that color within the circle.)

Figure 2.5 shows the possibilities for two shared attributes.

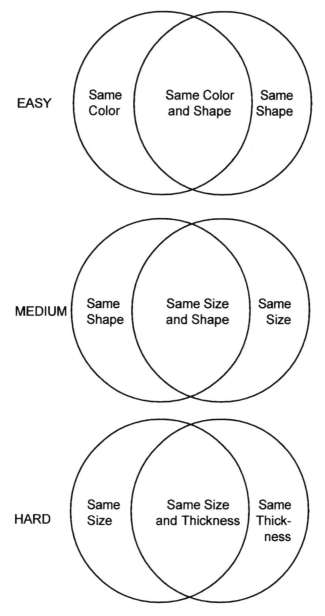

EASY

Same Color Same Color and Shape Same Shape

MEDIUM

Same Shape Same Size and Shape Same Size

HARD

Same Size Same Size and Thickness Same Thickness

Fig. 2.5.

Figure 2.6 shows one possible setup for a difficult activity.

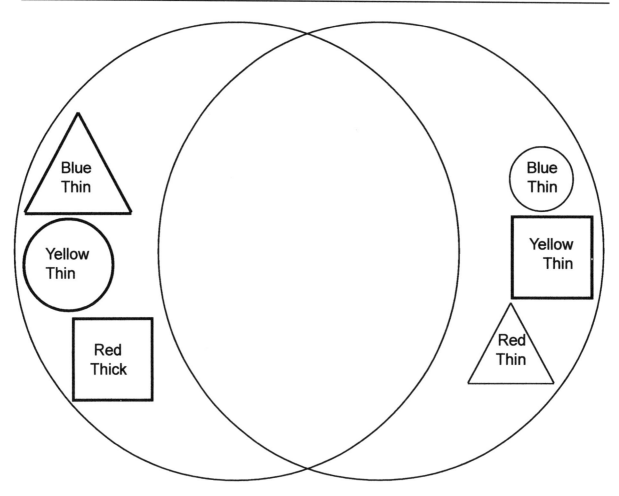

Fig. 2.6.

When complete, students will have placed the large, thin blue triangle; the large, thin, yellow circle; and the large, thin, yellow square in the overlapping center.

Figures 2.7 and 2.8 show the possibilities for three shared attributes. Figure 2.7 shows the possibilities when two circles are used.

Figure 2.8 shows the possibilities when three circles are used.

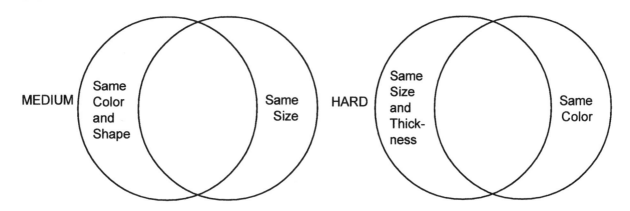

Fig. 2.7.

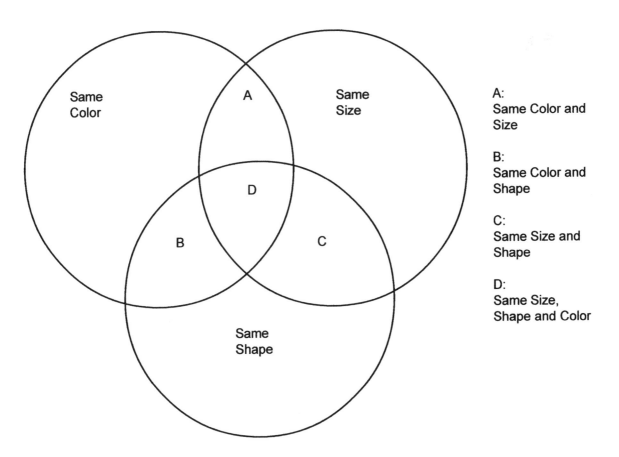

A:
Same Color and
Size

B:
Same Color and
Shape

C:
Same Size and
Shape

D:
Same Size,
Shape and Color

Fig. 2.8.

To add to the difficulty of the activity later in the year, the teacher can fill in one circle and the overlapping section and ask students what goes in the other circle. Finally, the teacher can fill in only the overlapping section and ask students what goes in each circle. This can be an individual warm-up activity at the beginning of the day about once every other week to get students quiet and thinking.

The Science Classroom

Any classification activity in science is ideally suited to the Venn diagram. A helpful focus through the student's reading is to look for similarities and differences and to fill in their chart during or after reading, viewing a tape, or listening to a lecture. Small groups can be formed to note similarities between two of many different groups being studied. For example, after studying the five senses students could be placed in five learning groups. One group could find the similarities between touch and the other four senses, one group could relate taste, and so on. The groups could come back together and, by compiling their information, deal with the higher-order thinking activity of describing how *all* five systems are similar.

The Social Studies Classroom

Venn diagrams can be used to compare different cultures, whether the difference is based on time, locale, economics, or political beliefs. It is a helpful review for past lessons to have students look for similarities and differences during readings, audio visual presentations, or lectures (e.g., students have recently studied rural life and are now reading about urban life). This helps focus students on the content area and makes the facts more pertinent.

Venn diagrams can be used to compare political leaders (past or present), politicians seeking office, political parties, events, or religions. They can be used to compare current events and historical events where there exist similarities and differences (e.g., the Holocaust could be compared with any present conflicts involving a feeling of ethnic or religious superiority).

The Music Classroom

The Venn diagram format can easily accommodate listening activities comparing the works of composers. Comparing the similarities and differences between different instruments in the orchestra could help students realize why instruction in one instrument is easily adapted to some but not all instruments. The Venn diagram can be used to compare the mood, rhythm, and melody of two musical pieces. Opera could be introduced to students by comparing it to familiar literature.

The Physical Education Classroom

When introducing a new sport to students, comparisons can be made to a familiar sport using the Venn diagram. This will clearly define what skills students already have knowledge of while indicating what new skills will be learned and what skills will not be necessary for this new sport.

The Art Classroom

Venn diagrams are useful in comparing the works of two artists or in comparing two works of one artist. They can help focus students on looking at more than just the whole picture—the technique, message, and mood of the work.

Venn diagrams are useful when introducing a new medium to students. As in physical education, this will clearly define what skills students already have knowledge of, what skills will be new, and what skills will not be used.

Assessment Opportunities

Students can use their charts in a pre-writing exercise in preparation for doing a paper comparing two concepts. Students can also use their charts to plan a presentation to the class about a subject. The chart itself can be part of the student's letter grade and will help the teacher know whether the student has an understanding of the assignment and the concepts being written about.

Figure 2.9 is an example speaking assignment for students on the presidents of the United States. Blanks within the example can be filled in with any number the teacher chooses.

The Venn diagram could be included in any formal assessment in two possible ways. The test can list attributes of the two concepts and ask the student to place them correctly into the diagram to test an understanding of similarities and differences. The student could be asked to list similarities and differences from their own memory or from visual assessment and place them correctly on the chart.

Figure 2.10 is an example of the second type, using a performance-based question for a science test. The skill being tested is observation. Included at the end of the chapter is a checklist for students completing this activity.

When observing students completing a Venn diagram, the teacher should note the process each student uses. Does the student complete one section at a time and move to another, focus on similarities first and then differences, or randomly fill out the diagram? This will provide the teacher with an awareness of how a student organizes and retrieves information. By asking students "Why?" concerning placement, the teacher can quickly and easily get students used to justifying their reasoning.

Speaking Assignment on Two Presidents

1. Choose two presidents of the United States.

2. Read a book on each one.

3. Use a Venn Diagram and fill in _____ ways they were similar and _____ ways for each in which they were different. (Worth 50 points)

4. Write out a speech, use notecards or memorize it, and present it to the class. (Worth 50 points)

5. The speech should tell who the president s were, how they were similar and how they were different. Be sure you stand straight, speak clearly, and keep us interested!

Fig. 2.9.

Look closely at the two bones on your table. The smaller one is a chicken bone and the larger is a turkey bone. Draw a Venn Diagram and list as many similarities and differences as you can observe. Use the checklist to guide you.

Fig. 2.10.

Checklist for Science Activity	Yes	No
1. Did you observe the bones?		
2. Did you list everything you observed about the chicken bone in this box?		
3. Did you list everything you observed about the turkey bone in this box?		
4. Does the far left circle contain traits that only the chicken bone has?		
5. Does the far right circle contain traits that only the turkey bone has?		
6. Did you write traits they share in the overlapping portion?		
7. Did you check everything again to be sure your Venn diagram is complete?		

VENN DIAGRAM

THREE

Frameworks for Webbing

What Are They?

Frameworks for webbing are a strategy to access and share prior knowledge. A simple outlining technique, they are especially appropriate when the topic being discussed has numerous subtopics. Generally, frameworks for webbing consist of a main topic, subtopics, and details (sometimes called support strands) about those subtopics. Traditionally used in brainstorming activities and to teach reading, writing, and social studies, they encourage thought regarding the whole and its parts.

Why Use Them?

Students will

- become actively involved in creating subtopics.

- visually focus on the parts belonging to each subtopic.

- actively restructure information into a simple and clear outline format.

- access and share existing knowledge and build bridges to future knowledge through brainstorming activities.

How to Use Them

Teacher models and guides:

1. Attach a large piece of paper to the wall.

2. Draw a large circle in the center of the paper.

3. Label it with the main concept to be discussed. (A good starting topic might be a character from a story that has just been read.)

4. Brainstorm concepts students have regarding the character and subtopic titles.

5. Draw as many subtopic circles as needed.

6. Connect subtopic circles to the main concept circle with lines.

7. Fill in the circles with information from brainstorming.

8. Brainstorm finer details and place these on lines drawn off of each subtopic circle.

9. End the modeling session with a discussion of the benefits of this form of organization.

Whole-Group

The teacher discusses a topic and writes it in the center circle. The class brainstorms and the teacher or a student records the information from the class. The class decides whether a subtopic and details should be included and where.

Small-Group

The group can be assigned an idea, concept, topic, or subtopic. Each student in the group chooses a different color of pencil, crayon, or marker. Each student records their ideas. The group agrees on where the idea should be placed. If agreement cannot be reached, the idea is written along the border. Each person signs the chart using their color (this helps the teacher know how much each student contributed to the framework). Groups come together and share information with the whole class either orally or by posting their chart. Discussion can be held about any differences or questions.

Individual

Each student draws a chart and identifies subtopics and details, placing information in desired positions. When completed, students share their frameworks with the whole class, a partner, use it as an outline for a writing assignment, or hand it in for evaluation.

Suggestions for Use

Using webs to teach main idea/detail is dealt with in chapter five. The following suggestions deal with other uses of webs.

Traditional Format

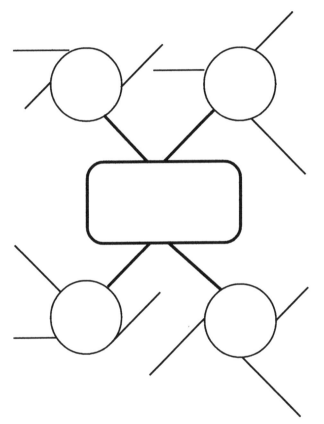

When introduced in the primary grades, the web should be in its simplest form—main topic and subtopics, but no details. Use very specific main topics (e.g., plants instead of living things).

In figure 3.2 the first-grade teacher supplied the topic "earth."

After the students read the chapter from the science textbook together, the teacher asked, "What can we see on the earth?" The students would then share responses. The teacher records and, as a class, the students brainstorm and come up with the categories. The reading from the book might not include some things that students thought should be included under the main topic. The teacher will need to decide whether to limit subtopics to the text or to include student generated subtopics.

Fig. 3.1.

The charts can be kept for a later activity that will teach adding details. The students will be paired off and each pair will be given a 3 foot length of string. The class will be taken outdoors and each pair will lay their string down in a circular shape in their own area. They will then observe their area and write in anything they see as details on their original framework. At this point students will need to include a category called "other." This is often necessary for those miscellaneous details that don't fit under any other broad subtopic. A completed chart might look like figure 3.3.

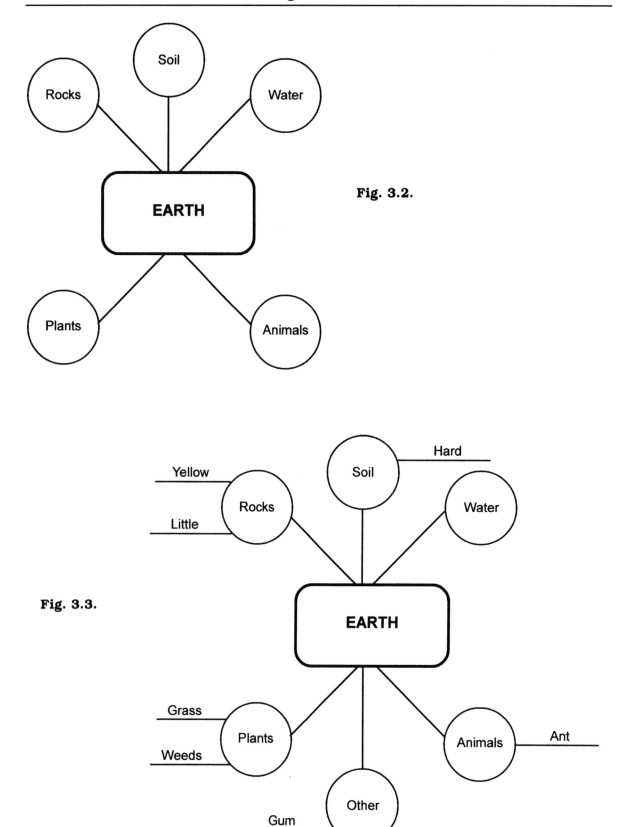

Fig. 3.2.

Fig. 3.3.

While their terminology won't be technical and the teacher may have to deal with phonetic spelling, this activity does encourage observation and is a concrete way to introduce detail. Student pairs might be given hand lenses for observing. This will add even more details. If the teacher doesn't feel the class is ready to work in pairs, a much larger string can be used and the whole class encouraged to look at the same circular area. Students would then share what they see and the teacher could record on the large class chart.

A character study using *The Three Little Pigs* provides another nice opportunity at the primary level to extend the chart to include details about the subtopics. The main topic is "The Characters in the Story." The teacher elicits from the students that the characters are the wolf, pig one, pig two, and pig three. Students can then brainstorm, as a class, traits and actions for these characters as illustrated in figure 3.4.

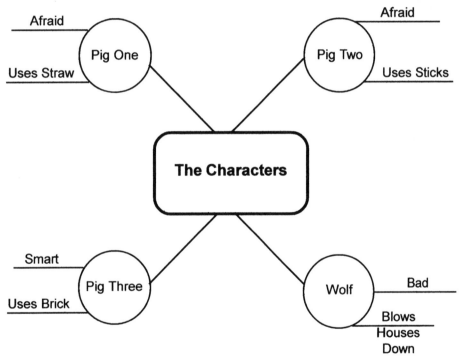

Fig. 3.4.

Students with significant experience using webbing or those in intermediate grades can be allowed to use the web in small groups or individually. At this level the students would benefit from webs that are used over several days or weeks. For example, during their study of the fifty states students could use figure 3.5 as a base web to do an in-depth study. The teacher would assign or allow students to choose two states to research. The student would then complete the details for each part of their web by using the encyclopedia, almanacs, and other resources.

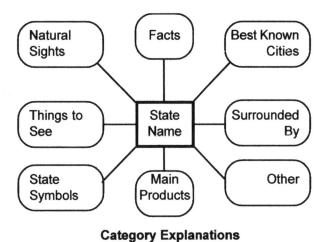

Category Explanations

FACTS: admission date, state admission
    number, population, area
BEST KNOWN CITIES: those cities with special
    historical or travel interest, capital
SURROUNDED BY: states, countries, or oceans
    that touch on this state's borders
OTHER: interesting facts that don't fit any other
    category
MAIN PRODUCTS: agricultural, fishing, mineral
    and manufacturing products from the state
STATE SYMBOLS: state bird, state flower, state
    tree, state motto, etc.
THINGS TO SEE: interesting historical or
    recreational sights
NATURAL SIGHTS: mountains, lakes, rivers,
    deserts, forests, etc.

Fig. 3.5.

As a concluding activity, students could do a presentation on their states, prepare an exhibit, or all webs could be put on display in the classroom or a display area in the school. If displayed, students could then take other classes, parents, or administrators on a tour of the web. The "web guides" would direct attention to the name of each state and facts that were included about it. In any long term project with an end of unit test, students could use their own copies as study sheets.

Outlining

The webbing technique is particularly effective in outlining a portion of reading material or in preparation for a writing assignment. By using it as an outlining technique, students do not become bogged down in the structure of the traditional outline format but can concentrate on logically making decisions about relationships. For example, students at the beginning of the year, might be given a writing assignment about how they spent the summer. As a group the class could brainstorm possible subtopics; i.e., travels, sports, readings, and so on. Students should realize that these subtopics need to be fairly general because they will be the main idea of each paragraph. Students might have different needs for subtopics. A student who visited several places during the summer might have a subtopic that just said "travel" with strand supports that listed each city. A student who only visited one city might have a subtopic naming that city with supporting strands about what was visited. Students then fill in their own web and use it to write their paper. (See figure 3.6) Left with minimal instruction the students will often end up with a paper that is just a listing of facts. To encourage creative expression, ask the students to include in each support strand some descriptive language that they might want to use in their writing; i.e., interesting planes, beautiful flowers, and so on. (**Hint:** If someone says they did not do anything during the summer and can't do the assignment, have brochures, menus, and so on available so they can write about a "Fantasy Summer.")

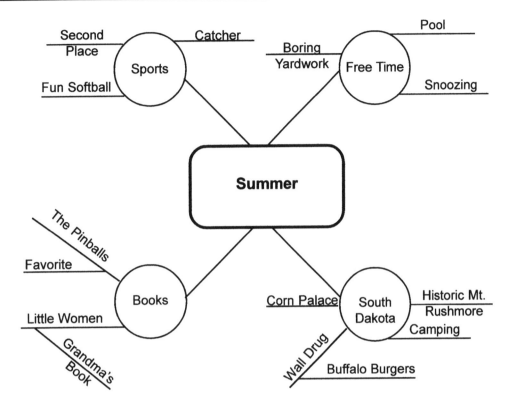

Fig. 3.6.

Vocabulary

Webbing helps in working on vocabulary from any content area. The main topic is the title of the story, chapter being studied in the textbook, or spelling lesson. The strand supports can be definition, descriptions, synonyms, or related phrases. Students could use this sheet as an introductory activity to the unit by filling in any information that might be in their background knowledge. The sheet can then be kept and worked on during or after the lessons. For example, a bulletin board can be made for math vocabulary. Using the web as a bulletin board utilizes not only its usefulness but keeps the vocabulary words in view for both teacher and student information throughout the unit. The main topic would be the concept being learned; i.e., addition, geometric shapes, ratio, and so on. The subtopics would be the vocabulary words from the unit. Prior to presenting the first lesson, the class could brainstorm and place on the board anything they know about the vocabulary words placed there. Students will also have a convenient reference for any unfamiliar words. Including an example or picture whenever possible will make this chart even more beneficial. An example from a third grade math unit is illustrated in figure 3.7.

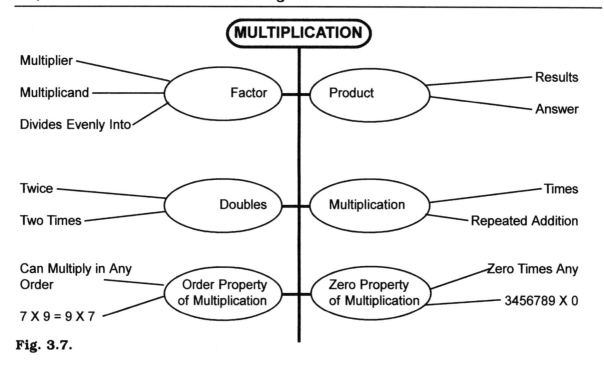

Fig. 3.7.

Teacher Lesson Plans

Teachers can benefit from using the web when trying to plan an integrated unit. The main topic will be the global topic around which all lessons will be organized. Each subtopic will be the units that will be taught from each subject area. Support strands off each subtopic will be individual lessons that will be taught in that unit. This will help ensure that individual lessons fit or are made to fit into the global topic. When daily lesson plans are made it will be clear which topics fit where. REMEMBER: Don't be afraid to change the order in your textbook. It's only a resource.

Figure 3.8 is an example of the main topic and subtopics for a teacher's integrated unit on "Colonial Days."

Fig. 3.8.

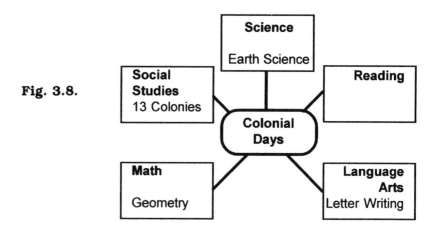

When the teachers fill in the details for each unit, they will add activities or a focus for the lesson that relates to the main topic. For instance, the math unit on geometry could include work with "patchwork quilts" as presented in *Garbage Pizza, Patchwork Quilts, and Math Magic* by Susan Ohanian. The science unit on earth science could focus on how weathering, energy resources, and pollution were dealt with in colonial times as well as in our time. The language arts lessons could include letter writing activities to a colonial character, from a colonial student, requesting information about a museum's colonial exhibit, and so on. By working off the web the teacher will always have the main topic as a focus.

Discussion Webs

Figure 3.9 is a typical discussion web.

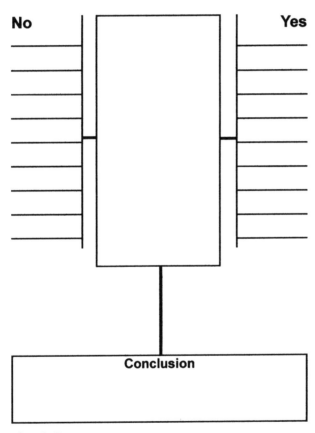

Fig. 3.9.

This web helps the student look at both sides of an issue before drawing a conclusion. First have the students do their reading, listening, or viewing of the lesson. Students will, individually or in pairs, fill in the YES–NO section of the discussion web with reasons or justifications. By filling this in individually they will start the discussion with an opinion of their own. Remind them not to fill in the conclusion section until after their group discussion. **This discussion is the most important part of the web.**

This web also lends itself to cooperative work groups. These groups meet, fill in the YES–NO section, and decide on a group conclusion. Students can be encouraged to circle the strong supporting arguments that helped them arrive at the conclusion. Each group then chooses a spokesperson to present the group's reasons and conclusion before the entire class. Students can write a short paragraph describing their conclusion. Individuals should indicate if this conclusion was a change from their thought prior to the group's discussion.

In figure 3.10 students were asked to pretend that they were Harry S. Truman and that they had to decide whether or not to drop the bomb. Students were reminded that good decision making involves looking at both sides of an issue.

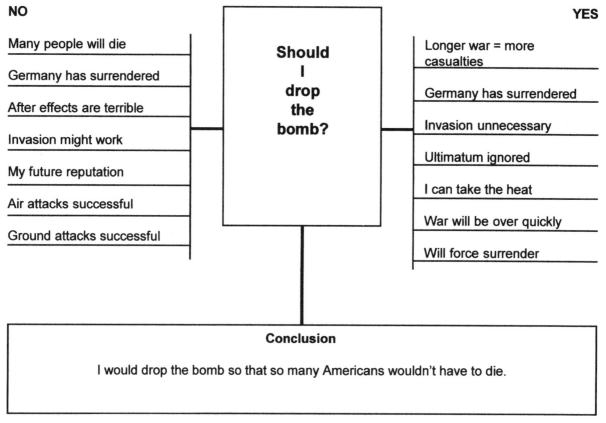

NO

Many people will die

Germany has surrendered

After effects are terrible

Invasion might work

My future reputation

Air attacks successful

Ground attacks successful

Should I drop the bomb?

YES

Longer war = more casualties

Germany has surrendered

Invasion unnecessary

Ultimatum ignored

I can take the heat

War will be over quickly

Will force surrender

Conclusion

I would drop the bomb so that so many Americans wouldn't have to die.

Fig. 3.10.

This is an excellent way to prepare students to debate topics on current issues in all subject areas. This format would also be useful to fill in during a "mock–trial" or while listening to a debate. The teacher would be provided with information about what the student heard and why they chose the conclusion they did. Students could also use this format as their outline for argumentative writing. The Discussion Web can help the student clarify issues for unbiased writing (i.e., a newspaper article). An interesting activity would be to have the students fill out a Discussion Web on a chapter in their textbook. Texts are supposed to be unbiased but an evaluation of them can indicate bias. Students can check their own writing for bias in the same way.

Discussion webs can also be used in the primary classroom. At this level it works best as a whole group activity. Topics to be discussed are varied but are often suggested by literature or teaching some of life's rules. After reading *How Big Is a Foot?* by Rolf Myller a web could be done asking if a ruler is best for measuring. After reading *Cloudy with a Chance of Meatballs* by Judi Barrett a web could be done discussing if food raining from the sky would be a good thing. Questions on hygiene or discipline can also be used. Figure 3.11 is a web for a discussion on class discipline in reference to hitting.

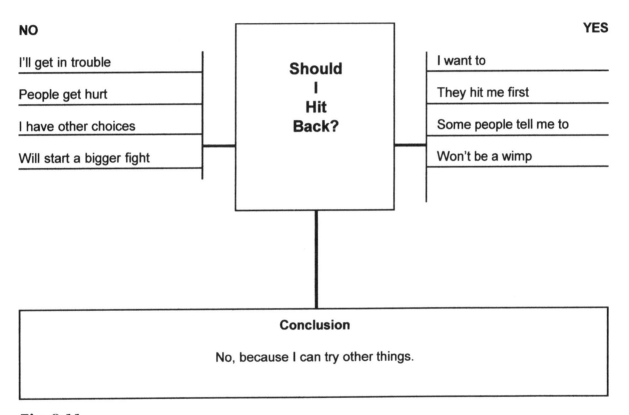

Fig. 3.11.

The #!#! TV

Discussion webs work exceptionally well with TV. Students can be asked to watch presidential debates, State of the Union messages, presidential news conferences, or tapes of informative news shows. A question of concern to the students or the local area can be pinpointed and students can record all information that is given on the topic. They can then form their own conclusion. Papers would be brought to class and an effective current events session would occur. Always keep in mind that the discussion following the filling out of this format is its most essential component. The format provides the students with a framework in which to record ideas and information in an organized way to use during discussions.

TREE FORMAT

The two choices are represented in figure 3.12.

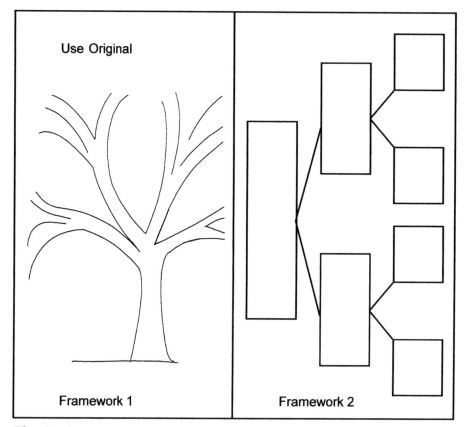

Fig. 3.12.

THE MATHEMATICS CLASSROOM

Framework one works well with topics that can be grouped into families. The following is a tree used to organize multiplication facts. The trunk is the main topic, the limbs are the subtopics and the branches are the supporting strands. Students are given the following information:

Main topic:	Multiplication
Subtopics:	Products—9, 10, 11, 12
Support Strand:	Multiplication problems with a particular product

The students draw or are given a tree with four branches and are instructed to place one of the products on each branch. the students then add a limb with an appropriate multiplication problem on each. This provides students with practice factoring numbers and can be used as a quick review, warm-up activity, or homework assignment. By changing the products the activity can be used over and over. A completed tree for this assignment would look like figure 3.13.

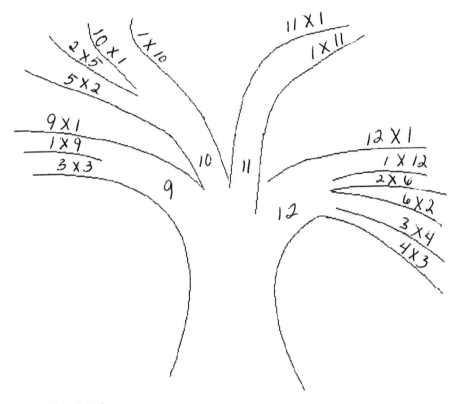

Fig. 3.13.

Framework one (fig. 3.12) would be useful when discussing any type of classification, such as animals, plants, and so on. An interesting tree could be developed using the twelve months of the year. Each limb could be assigned the name of a month and the branches could be facts about that month (i.e., days in the month, holidays in that month, class birthdays in the month, and so on).

Framework two (fig. 3.12) is a simpler tree format and is regularly used in probability. Figure 3.14 shows a tree for the following facts. A girl has two blouses, three jackets, and two skirts. How many three-piece outfits can she make? (B1 = blouse one, B2 = blouse two, J1 = jacket one, J2 = jacket two, J3 = jacket three, S1 = skirt one, and S2 = skirt two.)

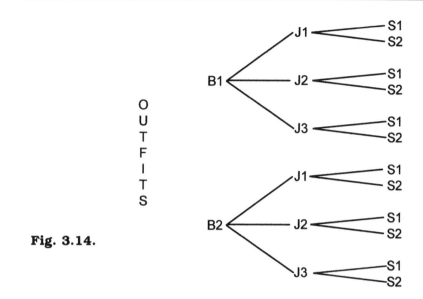

Fig. 3.14.

The combinations are read across connecting lines. For example, the first outfit would include blouse one, jacket one, and skirt one. The second outfit would include blouse one, jacket one, and skirt two. The third outfit would include blouse one, jacket two, and skirt one and so on for a total of 12 outfits.

This format could be applied to other curriculum areas as well.

The Reading Classroom

A partial character study of the two main characters in Pearl Buck's *The Big Wave* might look like figure 3.15.

Students could use this same concept as a pre-writing strategy when creating their own characters for creative writing assignments.

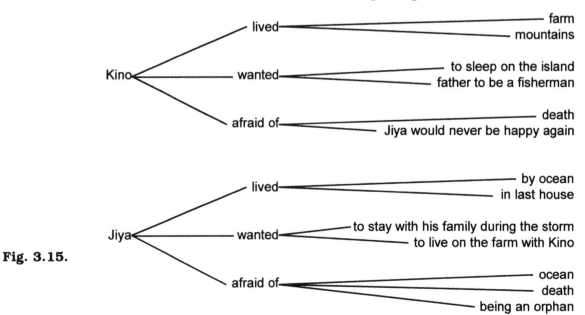

Fig. 3.15.

The Writing Classroom

Any of the formats can be used in the writing classroom. The web serves as an outline during pre-writing. It will help structure the student's writing into natural paragraphs and becomes a useful tool in teaching paragraphing. The brainstorming helps students generate ideas or topics to write about. When creating a character, the student can generate broad subtopics and then fill in details that substantiate these characteristics. This makes the character they write about fuller and more lifelike to their reader.

As a post–writing activity, the student can formulate an outline from their writing or about their character to check to see if all details included fit under the general idea of each paragraph.

The ability to form an extensive outline without worrying about the structure of a traditional outline makes this a very useful format for research papers. Students can take their global topic, brainstorm several subtopics and then begin to fill in the details from their research. (For example, the web described previously about collecting information on a state could be a springboard for a research paper.)

Assessment Opportunities

We just finished reading about Colin's hysterics in "The Tantrum." Fill out a Discussion Web answering the question:

> Was Mary wrong to speak so harshly to Colin?

Use your web to write a four paragraph paper. The paragraphs should cover:

1. Introduction

2. "No" reasons

3. "Yes" reasons

4. Your conclusion

Students can use their webs as an outline for writing assessments. The traditional format would work with most topics, but an argumentative topic would require the use of the Discussion Web format. The completed framework would be included in the grade.

Figure 3.16 is an example Discussion Web question for students who had just finished reading "The Tantrum" from *The Secret Garden* by Frances Hodgson Burnett. When grading this, consideration should be given to the completed framework, the four paragraphs, grammar, mechanics, presentation of both sides, a logical conclusion, and a natural flow to the overall writing. A suggested rubric is included at the end of this chapter.

Fig. 3.16.

Students can use their webs as an outline for a presentation to the class or to small groups. The web can take the place of note cards. Discussion Webs are especially beneficial in helping students look at both sides of an argument during formal or informal discussions and in the role playing of famous decision makers. A web could be filled out as an effective pre–debate activity for preparedness in meeting opposing arguments.

Any of the three formats could be used during formal assessment. A traditional web could be used during an "open note" test. ("Open note" test—A student's completed web would remain out for them to use when answering questions.) Students who failed to fill out a web or did an incomplete job would quickly realize the benefit of completing assignments.

The Discussion Web could be filled in as part of a formal test. For example, students could be requested to watch the news for a full week about a particular current event. At the end of the week they would be required to fill out a Discussion Web from the notes they had taken and from memory.

Figure 3.17 is an example question for the use of the tree format concerning the five senses. Students can draw their own tree or one can be provided. It is advisable to do an activity like this together before using it as a test question. Different types of questions will require different amounts of items already filled in. Note: Question 3 is from this teacher's expected outcomes from the unit and will vary by teacher.

Since there are 20 answers required, this can easily be converted to a 100 point test by scoring each answer as 5 points.

As the teacher observes students completing the frameworks, they should make note of the difficulties experienced and the order in which items are completed. When observing groups, check to be sure that all students are participating. Encourage groups to verbalize their reasoning. The teacher should ask:

Is this logical?

Is this reasoning supported by facts?

Is the student communicating clearly?

1. Draw a tree with five major limbs and four branches off each limb.

2. On each major branch write one of the five senses.

3. Write the answer to each of the following questions for each of the five senses. Write the answer on one of its four branches.

   A. Name one organ that uses this sense.
   B. Tell what this sense does.
   C. What is the name of a problem that could develop with this sense?
   D. Name one safety rule to follow to avoid problems with this sense.

Fig. 3.17.

Weighted Rubric	Possible Points	Earned
1. Framework completed.		
2. Included many good "No" reasons.		
3. Included many good "Yes" reasons.		
4. Well written presentation of both sides.		
5. Sound logical conclusion.		
6. Reasons given for conclusion.		
7. Grammar correct.		
8. Punctuation correct.		
9. Spelling correct.		
10. Entire piece flows very smoothly.		

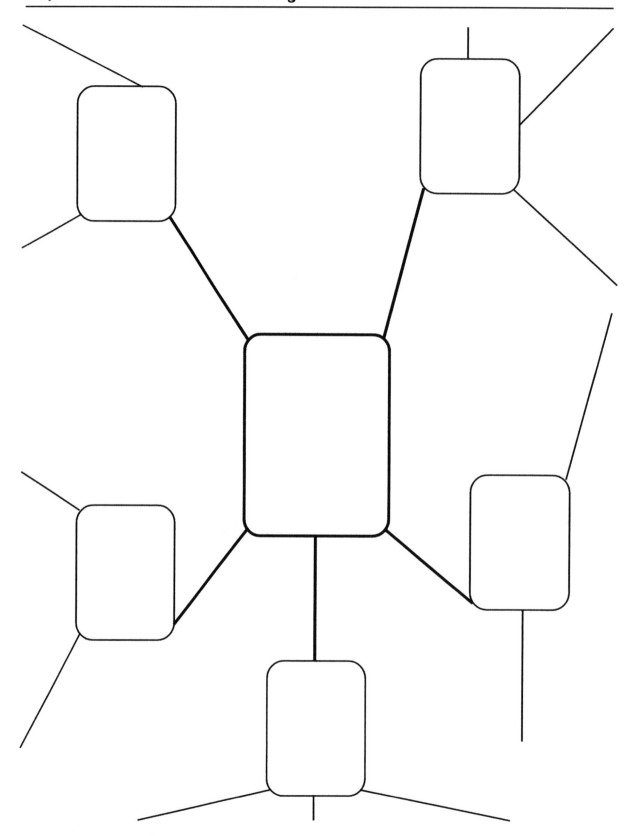

From *Creating Success in the Classroom!* © 1996. Teacher Ideas Press. (800) 237-6124.

No

Yes

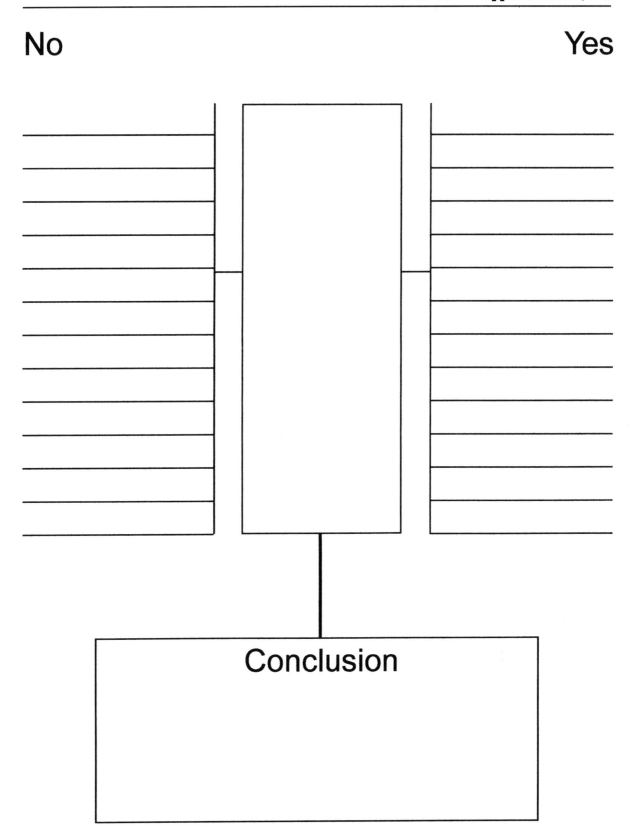

Conclusion

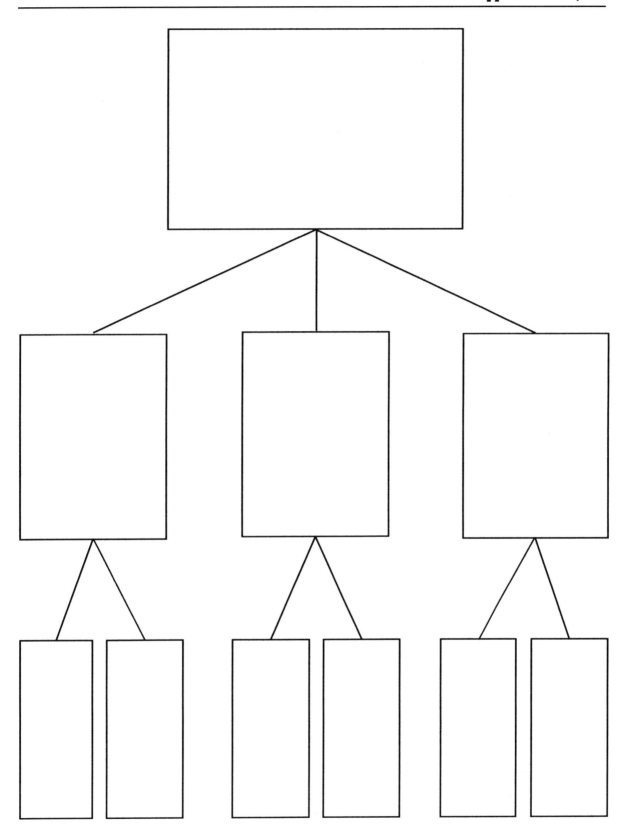

From *Creating Success in the Classroom!* © 1996. Teacher Ideas Press. (800) 237-6124.

FOUR

The KWL Frameworks

What Are They?

The KWL framework is a thinking strategy that taps prior knowledge before new information is learned. Traditionally used with expository text, this framework is used for constructing meaning based on prior knowledge and interest.

Why Use Them?

Students will

- become actively involved in setting purposes for reading, listening, viewing, or notetaking.

- actively engage in restructuring ideas while reading, listening, viewing or notetaking.

- become more focused while listening, viewing, or reading for specific information and show greater comprehension of the material.

How to Use Them

Teacher models and guides:

1. Brainstorming what is already known about a selected topic.

2. Recording prior knowledge.

3. Generating and recording additional information as needed.

4. Noting new information that is learned.

Whole-Group

The teacher or a student acts as a scribe and records information from the class.

Small-Group

Students brainstorm what they know about the topic while a recorder writes down the information. Students next decide what they want to know. Groups come together and share their information with the whole class. Students return to their small groups to gather additional information for a final whole-class report.

Individual

Each student identifies what they know about the topic. They determine and record what new information is desired. Next they record any new information learned. Finally, they share their information with the whole class or a homework partner.

Suggestions for Use

The traditional format is represented in figure 4.1.

K	W	L

Fig. 4.1.

This format lends itself to the study of content area and nonfiction material. The pretest has been used for years to try to glean prior knowledge from students. The devices used often gave limited information regarding each student. For example, there was no awareness of misconceptions a student might have regarding a topic. The KWL chart can be especially helpful in resolving the limitations of the pretest.

During the brainstorming session, allow students to include any and all information that they think they know under the "K" column, including misconceptions. It will be difficult at times to get some students to allow a misconception to be placed on the chart. For example, there are students who believe that *all* dinosaurs were ferocious, man-eating creatures. Other students in the class might be more sophisticated in their information and be aware that many dinosaurs were herbivorous. When controversy is raised during this brainstorming process, the matter can be settled by including a question mark next to the controversial statement, thus assuring students that the issue will be addressed. Students can also keep individual charts. Their individual chart will contain information in the appropriate columns. This allows students to keep track of their progress.

After brainstorming, lessons will have to be designed to deal with any misconceptions that students may have. In step 2 (above), students proceed, as a group or individually, to list in the "W" column additional information they want to know. The teacher provides opportunities for learning through media presentations, direct instruction, textbook study, research material, or trade books. These facts are recorded in the "L" column.

As lessons begin on the topic, facts gained can be used to verify information placed in the first column. Round, colored stickers can be placed next to each statement:

Red—if information was gained through reading.

Yellow—if information was provided by the teacher.

Green—if information was gained through experiments.

Orange—if information was gained through media material.

This practice models for children the essence of learning—validating information we know while combining it with new information.

As the "What I've Learned" column is filled out, the stickers could be placed by the new knowledge, indicating the source for that information. Students will begin learning how to take notes in an organized fashion.

Switch the Last Two Columns

In this format, students can tap prior knowledge through brainstorming. Students view or read material on the topic and record what they have learned. Each unit of study can then be closed with a listing of other things students want to know and assignments can be given. This is an excellent time to establish cooperative research groups. This step also encourages students to tap into additional reference material or trade books to locate answers for their "What I Want to Know" column. It provides a great opportunity for students to realize that reading is not only for pleasure but for gathering information.

K	L	W

Fig. 4.2.

Eliminate the Middle

K	L

Fig. 4.3.

This is now an effective tool for recording prior knowledge and knowledge learned. In the time crunch of many of our classrooms today—even though teachers would like to explore concept learning further—often there is not sufficient time to explore "What I Want to Know."

This format also lends itself to character study in literature. The teacher could ask students what they know about witches—read a story about a nontraditional witch such as

Strega Nona from *Strega Nona* by Tomie dePaola and record new findings about witches. Perhaps students are working on the theme "heroes." They can brainstorm all the associations they have for heroes and, as they read various books about heroes, record new knowledge gained.

As another example, the KWL framework lends itself to discussion of stereotypes. Scientists often are pictured as wearing white coats and glasses, ensconced in a laboratory with vials and jars. Students can record these stereotypical views and, as they read articles about various types of scientists, record new knowledge gained, knowledge that may change stereotypical views.

Genre studies can use this strategy as well. Students can list what they know and expect from fairy tales—read a collection of fairy tales and record any new knowledge of genre structure learned.

Eliminate the First Column

L	W

When little prior knowledge exists about a topic, the KWL framework can be used with a textbook or media presentation to provide some knowledge base for all students. After studying the topic, record what is learned and what students still want to know as a springboard for further research. Students will be encouraged to use a variety of reference materials or trade books for this research.

Fig. 4.4.

For example, after studying the Maya civilization in the social studies textbook, students can list what they learned under the "L" column, as in figure 4.5.

L	W
Lived in Mexico and Central America Mayan farmers raised more food than they needed Were great architects Buildings were like huge pyramids Some buildings were 20 stories high Were astronomers and mathematicians Discovered the concept of zero Had a calendar and written language Civilization ended after 1000 years	

Fig. 4.5.

Students then brainstorm and list the things they still want to know. These are placed in the "W" column, as in figure 4.6.

L	W
Lived in Mexico and Central America Mayan farmers raised more food than they needed Were great architects Buildings were like huge pyramids Some buildings were 20 stories high Were astronomers and mathematicians Discovered the concept of zero Had a calendar and written language Civilization ended after 1000 years	What did the farmers grow? How did the farmers live? Did they have religion? How were they ruled? How did they build the buildings? What did they do for fun?

Fig. 4.6.

Five topics can be formed from the "W" column: "Crops of the Maya Civilization," "Family Living in the Maya Civilization," "Religion of the Maya Civilization," "The Ruling System of the Maya Civilization," and "Architecture of the Maya Civilization."

Cooperative study groups are formed and students do their research from a variety of resources and report to the class. Figure 4.7 is a sample chart that a group reporting on the Ruling System used in an actual presentation.

The Ruling System of the Mayan Civilization

The ruler and the aristocrats ruled everyone in the land. The people were afraid not to obey them because they thought they were descendants from the gods. The society was organized into groups.

Ruler: Everyone was controlled by the ruler.

Aristocrats: These were the highest ranking members of the noble families. They controlled trade and commerce and filled all the top jobs in the society. They became priests and food suppliers. The batobs were the city administrators and belonged to this group.

Lesser Aristocrats: Lower ranking priests, scribes, traders, architects, and master craftspeople were part of this group. The ah cuch cab advised the batobs and were part of this group.

Common People: Farmers, laborers, craftspeople and domestic workers belonged to this group.

Slaves: This group was made up of people in debt, criminals, and prisoners of war. They performed domestic duties, worked in the fields and were used as victims in the religious sacrifices to the gods.

The civilization was ruled by fear. People were afraid of the ruler and the aristocrats and there was very little crime.

Fig. 4.7.

CHANGE THE LETTERS

The KLU chart is especially effective in organizing math lessons. The students thoughts are led through a progression of easily understood small steps and a reason for teaching them. This organizer encourages the teacher to teach math in a way that allows students to feel comfortable with mathematics. Students often believe that each math lesson is a whole separate series of steps that we must learn each day. They do not realize, unless told, that each math lesson is just adding a small building block of new information to previous information. The easiest way to illustrate this organizer's use is through a lesson.

K	L	U
What I Know	What I Learned	How It's Used

Fig. 4.8.

The lesson will be on adding near doubles (6 + 7 =, 4 + 5 =, 8 + 9 =, etc.). First, deal with what students already know when coming into this lesson, as in figure 4.9.

K	L	U
How to add What a double is Adding doubles		

Fig. 4.9.

The teacher helps fill out the "What I Learned" column during the lesson, as in figure 4.10.

K	L	U
How to add What a double is Adding doubles	Recognizing a near double Adding a near double	

Fig. 4.10.

After students are thoroughly comfortable with this new concept, the teacher fills out the last column, as in figure 4.11.

K	L	U
How to add What a double is Adding doubles	Recognizing a near double Adding a near double	Aid in remembering those memorized facts that you have forgotten

Fig. 4.11.

Allowing students to know that they already come into any math lesson with some knowledge, and that they are just going to learn one or two small things becomes more and more important as they advance through math topics.

ANOTHER LETTER CHANGE

K	N	L
What I Know	What I Need to Know	What I Learned

Fig. 4.12.

This is an effective organizer for the student writing an informational article, a research paper, or a "how to" article. Students list what they already know about the topic, what they need to know before writing the first draft, and what they learned by completing their research. This framework can then be used to help them organize and write their papers.

ASSESSMENT OPPORTUNITIES

Students can use their chart to write an informational article, documentary, newspaper article, or report about the subject. Students can also use their chart to plan a presentation to classmates about the subject. Students' written work or speeches should reflect their ability to construct meaning based upon their prior knowledge about a subject integrated with new information they have learned.

Many teachers use an open-book format for content area tests. Rather than use a textbook, students could use their individual organizers in the testing situation. This example test could occur at the end of a fifth-grade chapter on electricity. Students will have been told to retain each KWL chart throughout the chapter. The teacher can show them how to set aside a place in their notebooks or provide special notebooks or files for safekeeping of the sheets. Absent students should be instructed to get a sheet for lessons missed and to fill them out using the main class sheet or by having a homework partner help them.

Figure 4.13 is a suggested point system for using these charts as part of the testing.

10 points - KWL charts - Points for having all of them and having them completely filled out. By checking on this first, you will have your students prepared for the rest of the testing. Emphasize to them how important it is to retain information in an organized place in the room or in their notebook.

40 points - End of chapter formal open book test from publisher or teacher made - Students are allowed to use their individual KWL charts for each lesson to help them answer the questions.

50 points - Performance Based Assessment - Students are allowed to use their individual KWL charts to make an inference from the following drawing and then to set up an experiment that will check their inference.

Fig. 4.13.

Figure 4.14 is a performance-based assessment example for this test.

Look at the drawings below. Write an inference about the materials inside Bag A and Bag B. Plan, describe, and do an experiment that would help check your inference. You may use your KWL charts.

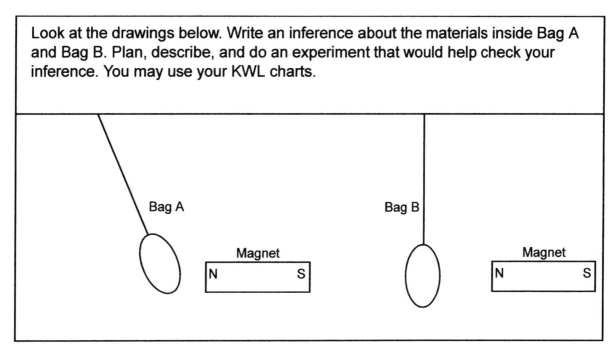

Fig 4.14.

K section	Do statements reflect true knowledge, hearsay or guesses? Are the statements clear and logical?
W section	Do statements reflect - recognition gaps in knowledge? - sincere and logical questions that stem from prior knowledge? - an extension beyond what is known?
L section	Do statements reflect new information accurately? Is the information restructured and recorded in student's own words?

Fig. 4.15.

If the framework is completed individually, the teacher can note how well the student organized his/her thinking in each section by using the questions in figure 4.15.

The ultimate goal—Upon completion, a student can state what he/she has learned from the lesson or unit of study. This could be done orally or written in a learning log.

WHAT I KNOW K	WHAT I WANT TO KNOW W	WHAT I LEARNED L

FIVE

Main Idea/Supporting Details
Frameworks

What Are They?

Main idea/supporting details frameworks provide students with a form to clearly identify the main idea of an article and its supporting details. They help students understand that most informative articles contain a few main ideas, then add details to further clarify and support the main idea.

Why Use Them?

- Once students can identify how information is organized in their reading material, they can better understand what they're reading.

- By turning the information into a diagram, students can see how one piece of information relates to another in an entire piece. Developing a framework is analogous to fitting together pieces in a puzzle. It shows the separate identity of each idea, as well as the part each idea plays in the total picture.

- When used as a notetaking tool, this framework clearly demonstrates to students how information is organized. It is a pattern guide, giving students a feel for what it means to recognize and use patterns of organization. This helps students remember and organize information in the same manner. Once completed, the student has a well-organized outline of what they have read.

- Notetaking also keeps the student more focused while reading and helps turn short-term memory into long-term memory.

- When used as a pre-writing activity, this framework helps students plan their writing piece around main ideas with details to support those ideas.

- As a post-writing check, students will diagram their own writing to make sure they have included main ideas and supporting details, and then revise, adding or deleting details as needed.

How to Use Them

Teacher models and guides:

1. Point out to students that information is often organized in a certain pattern when reading a piece of nonfiction material. Main idea/supporting details is one pattern of organization. In this pattern, one sentence or thought usually tells the main idea of a paragraph or a group of paragraphs. Sentences and phrases in those paragraphs give examples and details that support the main idea.

2. Read an informational article to students.

3. Ask students to recall details and examples that the article supplied.

4. List under the "Supporting Details" section on a class chart, an overhead, or the chalkboard.

5. Ask students to explain how all the details and examples fit together. Their answer should supply the main idea. If the main idea is stated in a sentence in the article reread the sentence or write it out.

6. Once the framework has been completed, demonstrate to students how they have restructured the information into an easy-to-read, easy-to-study format. After modeling this several times, add an additional step: have students write down what they have learned. This encourages students not only to record information but to process it and put it into their own words.

7. Repeat this procedure until students are comfortable. Be sure to include articles where the main idea is inferred or appears somewhere in the article other than the first or last sentence. Students often form the opinion that the main idea is the first or last sentence in a paragraph and will only look there when asked to identify the main idea.

Whole-Group

After reading as a whole group, individually, or in pairs, the teacher or a student acts as a scribe and records information on a class main idea/supporting details framework. The group then evaluates the chart to make sure all important information is there. The group should be encouraged to tell how each detail supports the main idea.

Small-Group

While reading, the members of the group record supporting details found in an article, textbook chapter, and so on. After reading, the group must reach consensus on the main idea. After a certain time period, the groups come together and share their frameworks with the class. This is a great way to have various groups reading different parts of a chapter. When the whole group assembles, each group is responsible for "teaching" their section.

Individual

While reading, each student independently fills out the framework. It is often a good idea for the teacher to furnish the main idea initially and allow students to add supporting details. After completion, students share their frameworks with a partner, a small group, the whole class, or hands it in for evaluation.

Suggestions for Use

Main Idea/Supporting Details Format

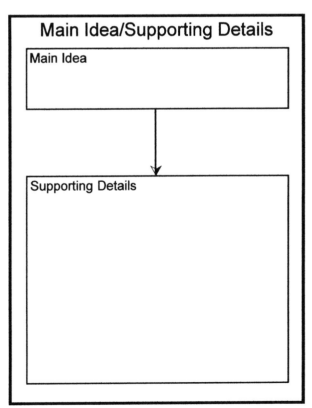

This framework is generally used with the reading, viewing, or listening of nonfiction material. It is imperative that students learn how to organize information from nonfiction material, beginning as early as kindergarten. Once a student enters fourth grade, most of the material he/she will interact with from that point on will be nonfiction. Many teachers report that students really struggle with absorbing and recording information from nonfiction sources.

This form can be easily reproduced on a large sheet of chart paper or on an overhead for whole-class sessions. Start with simple nonfiction passages, reminding students to look for details (facts) supplied.

Fig. 5.1.

For example, have a short paragraph on an overhead, chart, or reproduced for students:

> The loon has incredible strength. Loons can fly at speeds of more than 100 miles per hour. When a loon flies, its wings pump evenly, 260 times per minute. Loons are strong swimmers and propel themselves with webbed feet. A loon can dive to depths of 90 feet and can stay under the water for up to five minutes.

Ask students what details (facts) were given about loons. Make a list or highlight these:

incredible strength

fly 100 mph

wings pump 260 times per minute

strong swimmers

propel themselves with webbed feet

dive 90 feet

stay underwater for five minutes

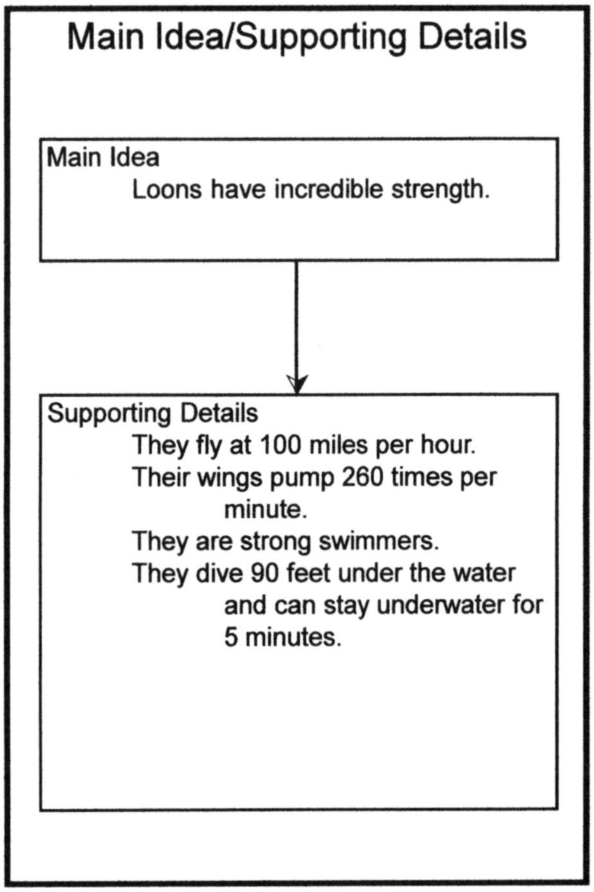

Main Idea/Supporting Details

Main Idea
Loons have incredible strength.

↓

Supporting Details
They fly at 100 miles per hour.
Their wings pump 260 times per minute.
They are strong swimmers.
They dive 90 feet under the water and can stay underwater for 5 minutes.

As you record the list, elicit from students what most of these details are reinforcing. Then complete the chart (see figure 5.2).

Encourage students to fill out the details first and then the main idea. This will help students see how the information is interconnected, rather than looking for the first or last sentence (as students often do when identifying main idea). When doing this activity with younger children, supply the main idea and, as you read to them, stop and ask them to give you a detail. When the chart is completed, have them discuss how each detail supports the main idea.

This same procedure can be used while viewing film strips and videos, or while listening to audio tapes. Initially, these may have to be stopped to allow students to record or dictate details. Work towards longer periods of viewing and listening as students' viewing and listening skills improve.

Fig. 5.2.

This form can be copied onto tagboard for students completing it individually or in a small group. This is an excellent strategy to prepare them for taking notes for research projects.

Older students, beginning research papers, can use this as their notetaking system. For example, a student is going to research "The Rise of Dictatorship Before WWII." This becomes the main idea on the card. The student then investigates to see who the dictators were.

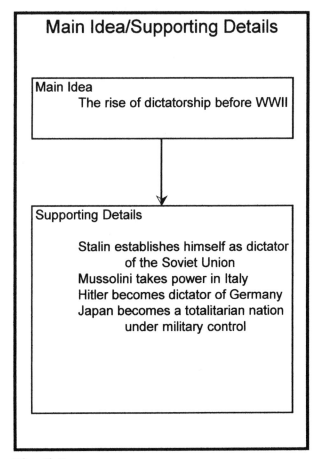

Fig. 5.3.

For further research, each supporting detail now becomes a main idea.

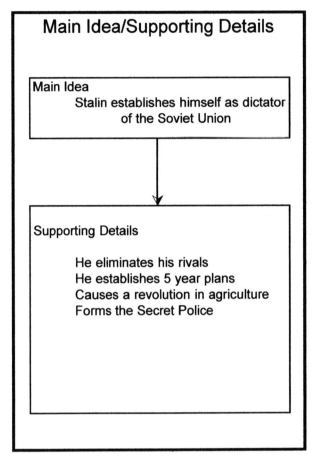

Fig. 5.4.

The student can now take the information from the cards and place them in an outline format. It is important that students see the organization of an outline and realize how titles in an outline are determined. This method, though time consuming, will clearly show the student how information should be organized in a research paper.

I. Main Idea I
  A. Major detail supporting Main Idea I
    1. Minor detail supporting A
    2. Minor detail supporting A
      a. Minor detail supporting 2
      b. Minor detail supporting 2
  B. Major detail supporting Main Idea I

I. The rise of dictatorship before WWII
  A. Stalin establishes himself as dictator of the Soviet Union
    1. He eliminates his rivals
    2. He establishes five-year plans
      a. Industrial
      b. Military
  B. Mussolini takes power in Italy

This helps the older student see the relationship between major and minor supporting details and what part they play in organizing a paper.

Music/Art Connection

This form can be used in music class. Introduce students to a ballad, folk song, and so on. Have the words on a chart or copied for students. Have them study the lyrics of a song to determine its theme or main idea; then have them explain how words and phrases from the lyrics support that theme (e.g., "Sama Kama Wacky Brown," words and music by George Goehring and Edward Warn).

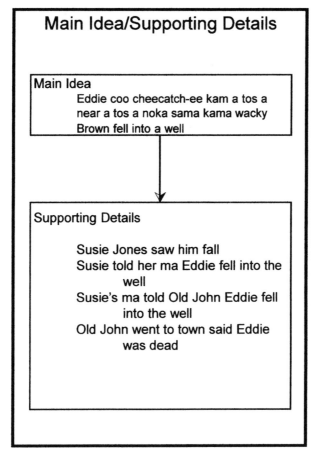

Fig. 5.5.

After students are comfortable with this, have them listen to a song (no lyrics copied) and fill out the framework. Have students design a record cover for a song that depicts the main idea of that song.

As another example, discuss an art print and have students list all the details they see in a painting and determine the main idea the artist was trying to convey from these details. Ask students to give the work a title that reflects the main idea. Share the title that the artist chose. Discuss with students if it reflects the main idea.

Give students a global theme (e.g., happiness). Have students draw a picture with a main idea that represents that theme. Students give it a title and fill out the main idea/supporting details framework. This is an effective way to introduce the concept of main idea.

Main Idea/Supporting Details Topic Format

Main Idea/Supporting Details

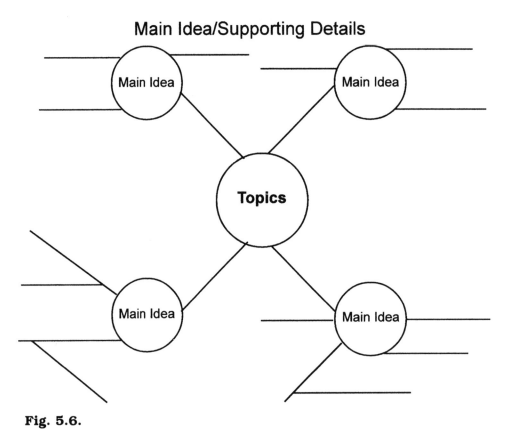

Fig. 5.6.

The topic format is very useful when studying a topic or theme that branches into subtopics (main ideas) (e.g., Communities). When studying communities, students will be investigating urban, suburban, and rural communities. Small groups can be assigned to read the material and come up with three supporting details for each of these main ideas. They can then present their material to the class and create a class main idea/supporting details "web." This is a wonderful way to introduce the class to a unit of study. Projects and further work can then branch off from the web.

The class framework may look like this:

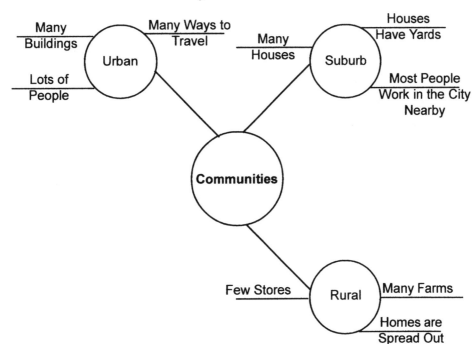

Fig. 5.7.

The different groups present their knowledge about the community they were responsible for. As a follow-up, groups with different memberships can be assembled to look into some of these details differently. One group may do Transportation, another group, Homes and the last group, Things to Do. They can use the same type of webbing to present their information:

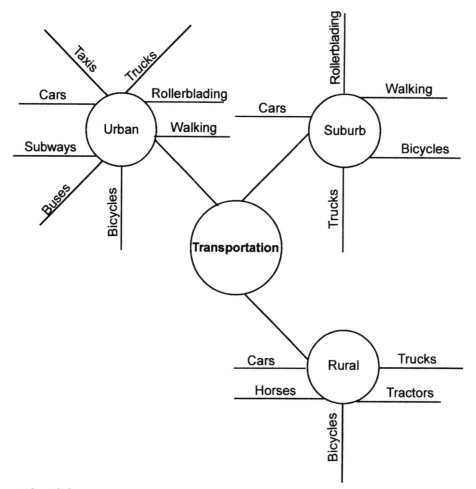

Fig. 5.8.

Students may present this framework to the class along with pictures or a mural. This is an activity that will prepare students for outlining and research in the future. It models for them a way to organize and present information.

This is also an effective framework to introduce students to a thematic unit. As study is completed on each main idea, details can be added to the framework. The framework will grow throughout the unit of study. When using this format, it is important for students to visualize how the information is organized around a theme. Use the terms "main idea" and "supporting details" often.

NOTETAKING FORM

Notetaking		
Paragraph or Page Number	Main Idea	Supporting Details
Summary		

Fig. 5.9.

This form is particularly useful when reading material from a textbook or encyclopedia article. Have students indicate what page or what paragraph they are reading—they may list supporting details and then list headings or they may use the headings from the textbook as their main idea.

Figure 5.10 is an example of a sixth-grader's sheet following the reading in a social studies text on the history of Japan.

So often, teachers assign reading from a text and ask students to answer the questions at the end of the chapter. Students often locate the answers to the questions and never read the entire chapter. This form forces students to process information in small chunks and record while they read. By writing a summary, students are asked to reprocess the information they just read into a more global statement. Students are encouraged to use the main ideas to help structure their summary. This technique will have to be modeled for students but will benefit them in the long run. A summary also becomes an excellent study sheet.

Notetaking		
Paragraph or Page Number	MAIN IDEA	SUPPORTING DETAILS
p. 490	Early Japan	country was not unified, people lived in clans, Yamato was leading clan, Shintoism was earliest religion
p. 491	Korea's Influence	Buddhism was introduced, brought ideas from China
p. 491	Prince Shotoku	welcomed Buddhist teachings, sent scholars to China - brought back art, writing, philosophy, government
p. 492	Feudal System	Samurai fought for lords, Shogun was supreme general of army, Yoritomo, a famous samurai, became Shogun - a dictator
p. 494	Matthew Perry	asked Japan to open doors to trade, signed treaty, adopted technology from West, became industrial leader of world in 20 years
p. 494 p. 495	Military Power	Japan wanted to create an empire, by 1942 controlled most of East Asia, bombed Pearl Harbor, U.S. dropped bombs, most of East Asia freed by end of WWII

Summary
   Japan's early people lived in clans and practiced Shintoism. They borrowed many ideas from the Chinese, especially Buddhism, writing, and government. Matthew Perry's visit caused Japan to become an industrial leader. Japan was a strong military power until the end of WWII.

Fig. 5.10.

Two Subject: Main Idea/Supporting Details

This is an excellent form to use when studying two or more subjects under the same topic. This can be used when students need to compare, contrast, or see differences among two different subjects under the same main idea.

Figure 5.11 is a comparison of two Native American cultures.

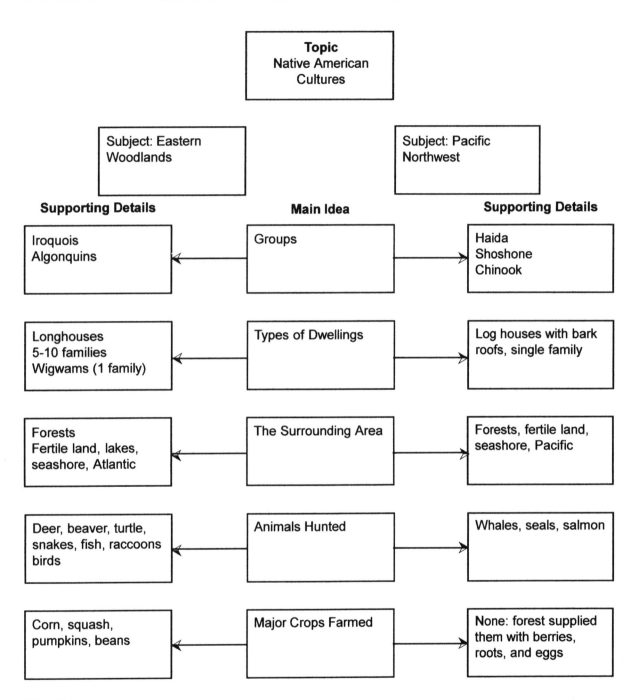

Fig. 5.11.

This not only reinforces how information is organized but provides a framework for students to write comparison/contrast paragraphs. This also provides a good form to take notes during a lecture that is organized around main points and compares two different subjects. Encourage students to be brief, and remind them that this framework serves as an outline. The possibility for using this chart crosses all areas of the curriculum:

Art—paintings, artists, mediums, tools

Gym—games, sports

Library—authors, books

Music—composers, songs

Science—planets, habitats, animals

Language—writing styles, genres

Mathematics—word problems, geometric shapes

Television—programs, content, advertisements

Social Studies—political figures, parties, communities

The Writing Classroom

Any of the frameworks presented can be used in the writing classroom. Most forms of writing center around a main idea supported by details. Once students understand and internalize the form, their writing will be clearer. Have students use the framework as a pre-writing organizer or a post-writing check. If used as a pre-writing organizer, even very young children can relate and begin putting main ideas into a paragraph format. If used as a post-writing check, it should be used in the revision stage.

Descriptive Paragraph:
    Main Idea—What are you describing, what feeling are you trying to establish?

    Supporting Details—What descriptions will reinforce and help your reader visualize and "feel" what you are describing?

How-To Paragraph:
    Main Idea—What are you explaining how to do and what do you expect your reader to know?

    Supporting Details—What steps must your reader take to accomplish this?

Persuasive Paragraph:
    Main Idea (Point of View)—What are you trying to persuade your reader to think about?

    Supporting Details—What arguments and facts can you use to support your idea/belief?

Newspaper Article:
    Main Idea—What is the subject of the article?

    Supporting Details—What supports the subject and helps the reader understand more clearly the information in the article?

Poem:

Main Idea—What subject, mood, or feeling are you trying to describe?

Supporting Details—What words and phrases will describe or help the reader to identify with your main idea?

The #!#! TV

Any of the frameworks can be used with television viewing. Do not switch the headings; just add descriptors to clarify what we are talking about. The main idea can be the main message in a program or advertisement. Supporting details are the visuals and auditory effects the producer uses to support that message. View a commercial together, and then ask students:

What is being sold?

What is the main idea (main message) they are trying to convince the consumer of?

How do they support this idea?

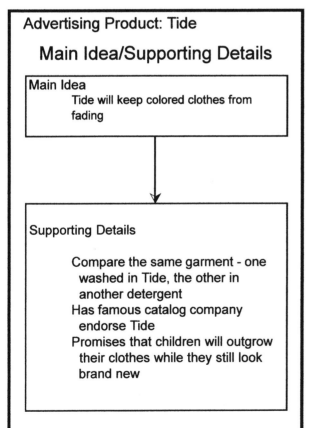

Advertising Product: Tide

Main Idea/Supporting Details

Main Idea
    Tide will keep colored clothes from fading

Supporting Details

    Compare the same garment - one washed in Tide, the other in another detergent
    Has famous catalog company endorse Tide
    Promises that children will outgrow their clothes while they still look brand new

Fig. 5.12.

ASSESSMENT OPPORTUNITIES

Main idea/supporting details frameworks deal with how information is organized. Our goal in teaching students to recognize main idea/supporting details should be to help students:

- to better understand the material they have read,

- to become proficient notetakers—organizing information into a well-organized outline,

- to plan their writing in a pattern of organization that will make their writing clearer and easier to understand, and

- to effectively evaluate their own writing and recognize how they have organized their thoughts.

When evaluating the student use of main idea/supporting details frameworks, it is important to keep in mind the *intent* of using the framework. It is not sufficient that a student correctly identifies main idea and supporting details. We must evaluate whether the student has a better understanding of what is read because of this recognition. The most effective way to evaluate this is to ask the student to recall verbally or to record in writing what they have learned after using the frameworks. If their recall reflects all of the main ideas (major points) and some details, the student is showing good use of the framework.

For example, copy a nonfiction passage and have the student highlight the main idea and supporting details. Have the student put the piece away and write down what he/she just read. Evaluating this should point the teacher in the direction instruction needs to go.

As a notetaking strategy, teachers must ask themselves during the evaluation:

Does the student determine the main idea correctly?

Can the student list supporting details in his/her own words?

Can the student discriminate between major and minor supporting details?

Can the student write or retell in his/her own words an effective summary?

Perhaps the most important reason for teaching this form of organization is to help students use it in their own writing.

As a pre-writing organizer, students must ask themselves:

What is my topic?

What are some things (main ideas) about my topic I want to talk about?

What details, reasons, examples, or explanations can I give to each main idea so my reader really understands what I am writing about?

These questions can be placed on a checklist (to be used with single or multiple-paragraph paper) for students, peer evaluators, and teachers to use before the first draft is written. (See Pre-write Checklist on page 88.) If used as a post-writing check, it should be used in the revision stage.

Students must ask themselves:

Is my main idea clear?

Do my details support the main idea? Did I include reasons, examples, description, or explanations?

Should I add more details to help the reader better understand my main idea?

Have I added too many details? Should I delete some details?

Does each main idea have its own paragraph?

Will the reader clearly understand what I am talking about?

These questions can be found in the form of a checklist (See Revision Check Sheet, page 89.) to be used before the final copy is produced. Students should be adding or deleting details to create clearer meaning.

After the student's final copy is produced, students should evaluate their own writing using one of the frameworks. The teacher should see students clearly identifying main idea and supporting details.

Our ultimate goal should be that all students learn to recognize this pattern of organization and apply it to their notetaking and writing strategies.

Name: _____	Pre-write Checklist		
Questions: Check if answer is Yes	Self	Peer	Teacher
Do I have a topic?			
Do I have main ideas about my topic I want to write about?			
Do I have:			
Details			
Reasons			
Examples			
Explanations			
About each main idea?			
I am ready to write my first draft.			
I need to know more details about my main idea before I write.			

Name: _____ Revision Check Sheet			
Questions: Check if answer is Yes	Self	Peer	Teacher
Is my main idea(s) clear?			
Do my details support the main idea? Did I include reasons, examples, descriptions, or explanations?			
Should I add more details to help the reader better understand my main idea?			
Have I added too many details? Should I delete some details?			
Does each main idea have its own paragraph?			
Will my reader clearly understand what I am talking about?			

Main Idea/Supporting Details

Main Idea

Supporting Details

Main Idea/Supporting Details

Main Idea

Supporting Details

Notetaking

Paragraph or Page Number	Main Idea	Supporting Details

Summary

Main Idea/Supporting Details

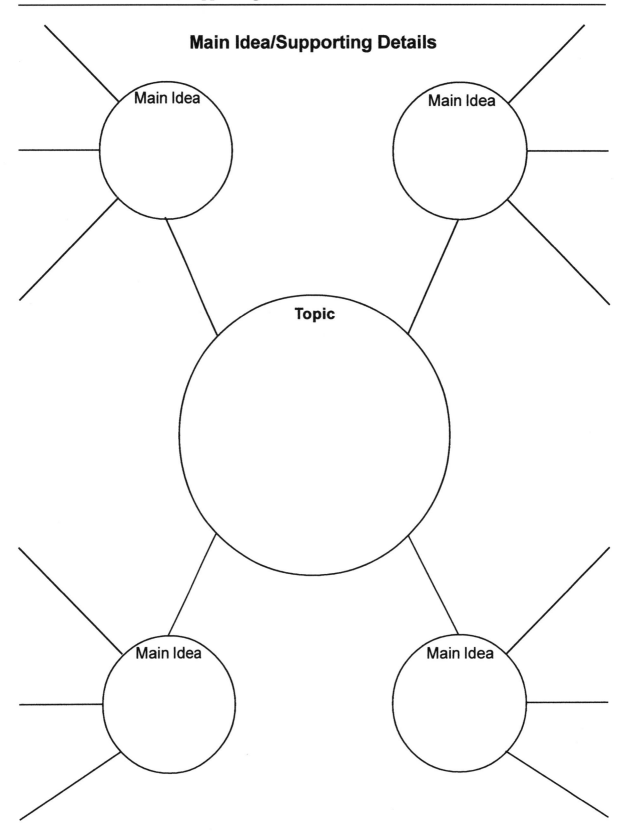

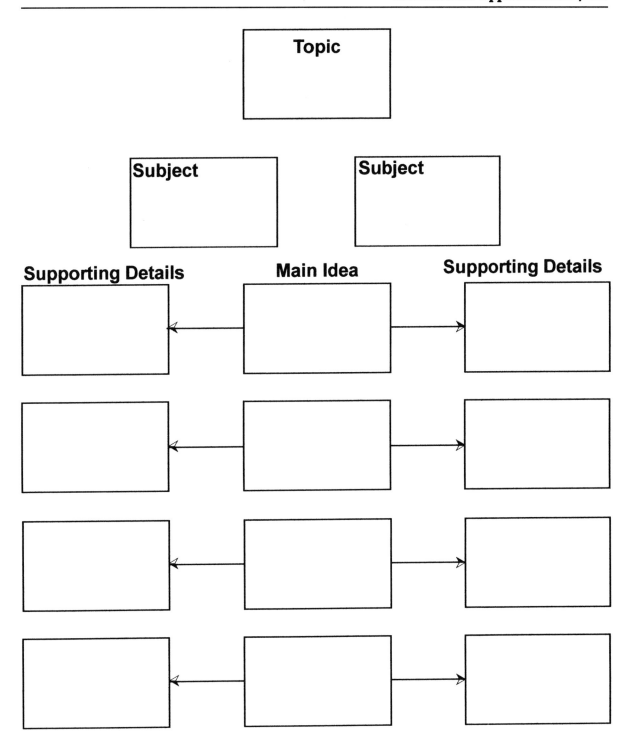

SIX

Cause-and-Effect Frameworks

What Are They?

Cause-and-effect frameworks provide students with a form to visually show the relationship between events. These frameworks are appropriate for looking at the effect or effects of an event or for looking for the cause or causes of an event. Traditionally, they are used in reading and social studies.

Why Use Them?

Students will

- become actively involved in recognizing the effect of an event while viewing, listening, reading, or notetaking.

- become actively involved in recognizing the cause of an event while viewing, listening, reading, or notetaking.

- actively restructure information into a simple format to highlight the cause and effect while reading, listening, viewing, or notetaking.

- visually focus on the number of causes of an event or the number of effects from one cause.

- detect the structures of stories and of expository text.

- write structured stories and expository text.

- plot sequence of events.

94

How to Use Them

Teacher models and guides:

1. The teacher or a student draws the framework and acts as a scribe, recording information from the class.

2. The teacher reads aloud a selection with many examples of causes and effects. (*The True Story of the Three Little Pigs* by Jon Scieszka is an excellent selection for any grade level.)

3. Students recall events.

4. The class brainstorms about whether it should be a cause or an effect and records this in the appropriate area.

5. The class decides the effect if the event was a cause or the cause if the event was an effect.

Whole-Group

The teacher identifies an effect and the students brainstorm and identify the cause. The teacher records it. The teacher identifies a cause and students brainstorm and identify the effect. The teacher records it. The teacher asks students to identify an event that is an effect and records it. The students then identify its cause and the teacher records it. The teacher asks students for an event that caused something else to happen and records it as a cause. The students identify the effect of the event and the teacher records it as an effect.

Small-Group

The group can be assigned a portion of a story, event, or topic. The group uses any of the frameworks appropriate to their story, event, or topic. (The teacher may decide on the framework with younger or inexperienced students.) The group can recall events and decide if they are causes or effects. All groups come together and share information with the whole class, either orally or by posting their charts. Discussion can be held about any questions or concerns.

Individual

The student identifies an event and decides if it is a cause or an effect. The student identifies the corresponding cause for an effect or effect for a cause. He/She places them correctly on a chart assigned by the teacher or, if experienced enough, on a chart of his/her choice. The student shares with the whole class, a partner, or hands it in for evaluation.

Suggestions for Use

Effect-and-Cause Format

The effect-and-cause format is represented in figure 6.1.

```
┌──────────┐          ┌──────────┐
│          │ Because  │          │   Fig. 6.1.
│          │          │          │
└──────────┘          └──────────┘
```

Students have more difficulty expressing cause and effect when they start with cause. In this simplest format, advantage is taken of their natural inclination to tell what happened followed by a "because." This is the ideal place to start with primary children in beginning to sort out the structure of any type of writing, but its simplicity allows for continued use with older students.

Because most reading tasks ask students to identify cause first, figure 6.2 can be used to reinforce this.

```
┌──────────┐          ┌──────────┐
│          │   So     │          │   Fig. 6.2.
│          │          │          │
└──────────┘          └──────────┘
```

A natural starting place would be with literature. In figure 6.3 students have just finished reading *Move It!* by Deborah Eaton. Students must decide on the cause.

```
┌──────────────┐              ┌──────────┐
│ The kids used│   Because    │          │   Fig. 6.3.
│ their pull   │              │          │
│ toys.        │              └──────────┘
└──────────────┘
```

In figure 6.4 the cause is given to 7 students and they supply the effect.

```
┌──────────┐          ┌──────────────┐
│          │ Because  │ They needed to│   Fig. 6.4.
│          │          │ move lots of  │
│          │          │ clothes.      │
└──────────┘          └──────────────┘
```

Finally, by leaving both boxes blank, the teacher asks students to supply both, as in figure 6.5.

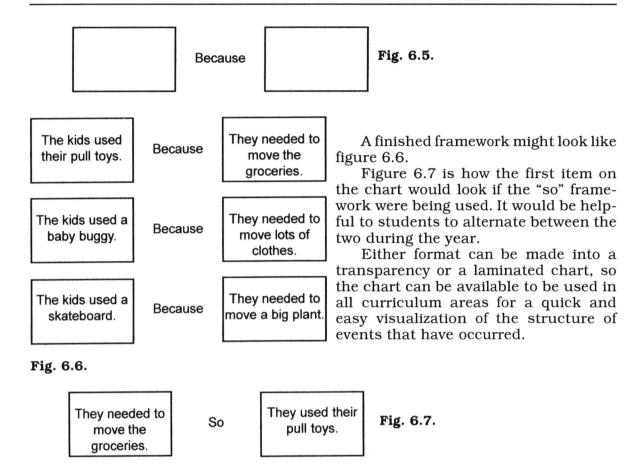

Fig. 6.5.

A finished framework might look like figure 6.6.

Figure 6.7 is how the first item on the chart would look if the "so" framework were being used. It would be helpful to students to alternate between the two during the year.

Either format can be made into a transparency or a laminated chart, so the chart can be available to be used in all curriculum areas for a quick and easy visualization of the structure of events that have occurred.

Fig. 6.6.

Fig. 6.7.

The Science Classroom

Steps for the science experiment used:

1. Divide the class into two groups of equal number, Group A and Group B.

2. Ask one student from each group to touch colored chalk dust (red is best).

3. The Group B person washes his/her hands; the Group A person does not.

4. Each of these students then shakes the hand of the next person in the group (make sure they use the hand that touched the chalk dust) and that person shakes the hand of the next and so on and so forth.

5. Every person in both groups is given an individual hand-wipe to wipe off their hand.

6. The wipes are examined with a hand lens to search for traces of the colored chalk.

7. Traces of chalk will be found on the Group A wipes but not on Group B.

The object of the experiment is to show how germs travel through the touch of unwashed hands. A cause-and-effect framework that might develop from this experiment is represented in figure 6.8.

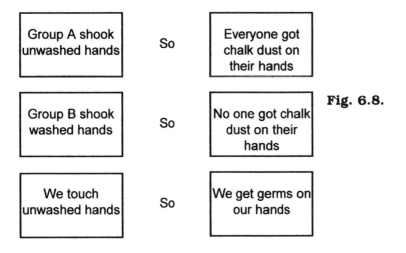

Fig. 6.8.

Social Behavior

Students need to realize that changing the cause is necessary to change a negative effect. This can be pointed out by using this chart at the beginning of the school year when we are determining our class rules. Ask students to brainstorm both good and bad things they have seen happen on the playground or in the classroom, as in figure 6.9.

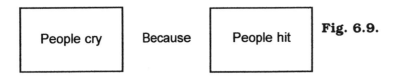

Fig. 6.9.

The teacher should elicit from students whether the effect is desirable or undesirable. When it is undesirable, the class can brainstorm what needs to be done to change the cause to get the desired effect. A rewrite of the above example might look like figure 6.10. This new cause and effect can become a class rule.

Fig. 6.10.

This simplest format lends itself well to anything with results that need to be changed. For example, in a typical primary class playing kickball for the first time, students leave their positions and all run after the ball. The physical education instructor can stop the action and discuss the negative effects of students leaving their positions. Discuss positive steps (causes) to reach the desired effect.

The Mathematics Classroom

In mathematics, we always think of the cause (the actual problem) first. After working the math problem 2 + 3 = 5, the teacher might write 2 + 3 in the cause box and ask for the effect, expecting a response of 5. A unique way to help reinforce fact "families" would be to fill in the boxes as in figure 6.11.

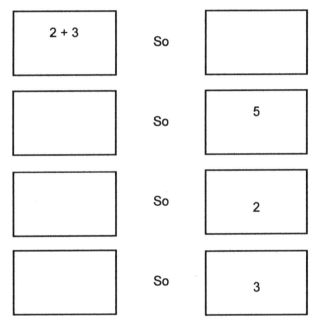

Fig. 6.11.

Initially, this chart would need to be filled out as a whole group activity so that students know what you want. Later, one of these could be on the overhead, on the chalkboard, or copied for them to complete as a warm-up activity at the beginning of the day or math class period.

Students would complete the chart as in figure 6.12.

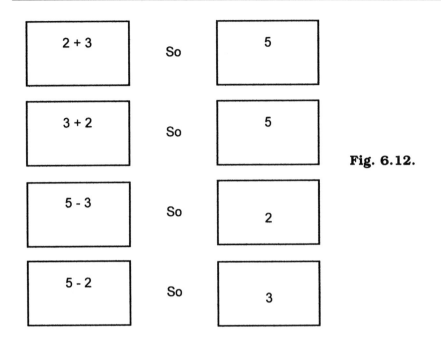

Fig. 6.12.

Cause-and-Effect Chains

Two choices are represented in figure 6.13 and figure 6.14.

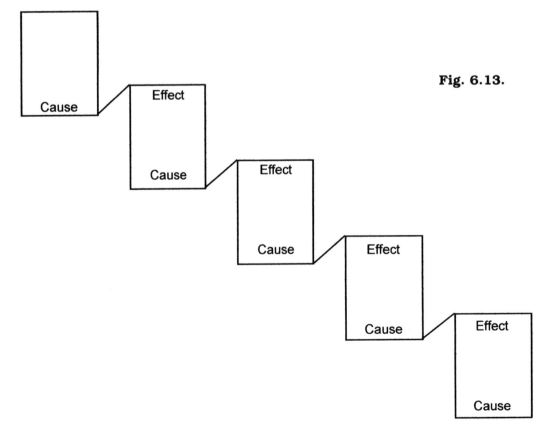

Fig. 6.13.

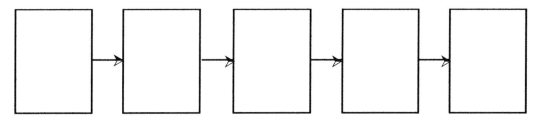

Fig. 6.14.

Both cause-and-effect chain formats show that an effect becomes a cause in some structures. This format allows students to plot out the structure of a story such as *Charlotte's Web* by E. B. White (see figure 6.15).

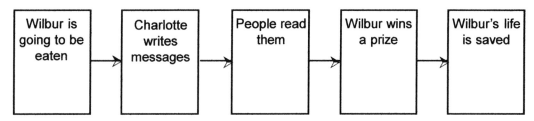

Fig. 6.15.

The Science Classroom Revisited

In science, the cause-and-effect chain could be used to illustrate life cycles such as those of the butterfly (see figure 6.16).

Older students working on becoming young inventors could do a Rube Goldberg contraption using the cause-and-effect chain format. *Webster's Dictionary* tells us a Rube Goldberg is "a device or method to accomplish by extremely complex and roundabout means a job that actually could be done simply." Students are, therefore, assigned a simple task and asked to create a contraption that is extremely complex. For example, the task is to crack an egg. The cause-and-effect chain format might look like figure 6.17.

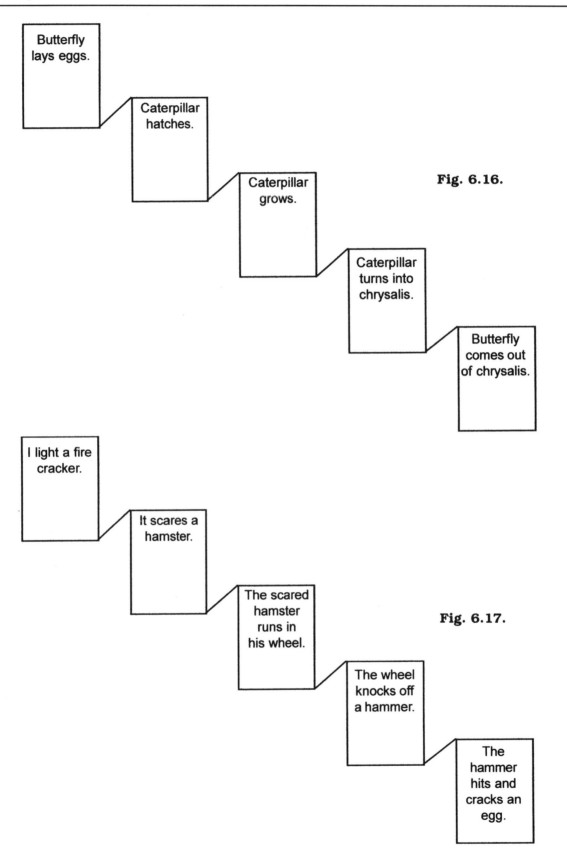

Butterfly lays eggs.

Caterpillar hatches.

Caterpillar grows.

Fig. 6.16.

Caterpillar turns into chrysalis.

Butterfly comes out of chrysalis.

I light a fire cracker.

It scares a hamster.

The scared hamster runs in his wheel.

Fig. 6.17.

The wheel knocks off a hammer.

The hammer hits and cracks an egg.

The Mathematics Classroom Revisited

In mathematics we see a chain of events in any problem with more than one step in solving (see figure 6.18).

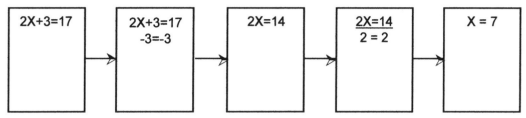

Fig. 6.18.

The #!#! TV

The cause-and-effect chain format can be used during television viewing to help students identify the main plot of a show. Most scripts are written on the basis of a chain of events. When the first event occurs, it is written in the chart. When its immediate effect is known, that is written, and so on throughout the show.

Students return the next day with their charts filled out, prepared to share and formulate a large class chart. The teacher could then propose the question, "What would have happened if (*an event in the storyline*) had been different?" Students could brainstorm about what the effect on the plot such a change would make. A follow-up writing activity would ask students to choose some event in this show, change it, and then discuss where that would have taken the characters. Naturally, when asking students to view a television show, care should be taken to choose a show that will inspire discussion but will not offend any of your students or their parents. An after school special aimed at a topic of interest to your community would be an excellent choice.

ONE CAUSE/MANY EFFECTS FORMAT

This format is useful during science experiments with unpredictable results. The teacher records the experiment as the cause and each different result can be documented as an effect. For example, students create and fly "loop airplanes." Everyone uses the same directions. Each student's airplane flies a different distance. The cause is "creating and flying the airplanes." The effect is the record of the different distances flown.

In history, one cause has also created different effects. Figure 6.20 is an example from a study of the Civil War using four different states that were part of the Union at that time.

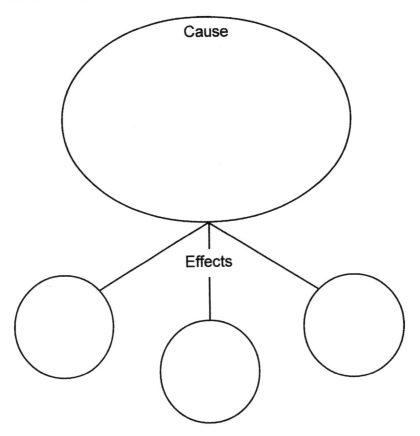

Fig. 6.19.

The chart gives students a visual look at different reactions to the same event. This same thing occurs in literature and on television. Using this chart to graphically display these occurrences will enhance students' learning.

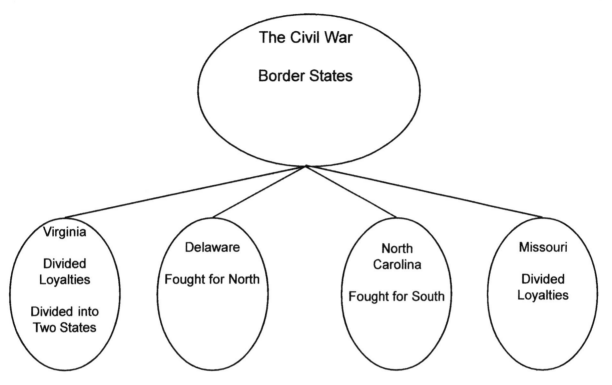

Fig. 6.20.

Many Causes/One Effect Format

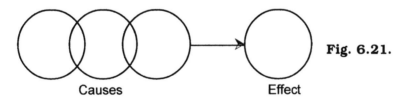

Fig. 6.21.

In this format there are several unrelated events that when taken together have one effect. A prime example of this is geometric shapes. A great activity would be to list the effect (the name of the shape) and have the students give the causes. Three completed examples are shown in figure 6.22.

Care should be taken to point out to students that this is not a cause/effect chain because one event: "all sides equal" does not cause the other event—"all right angles." You can have all sides equal without all right angles but then you have a new effect called a rhombus or an equilateral triangle, for example, depending on your third cause.

This format is available for other curriculum areas also. A scientific experiment often follows this format. The causes are the independent steps in the experiment. The effect is the result of the experiment.

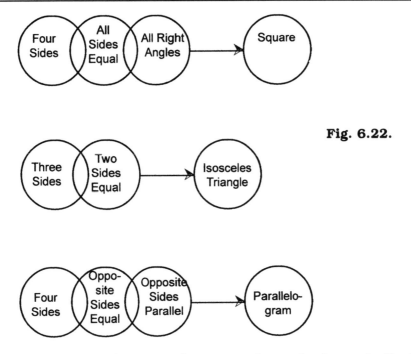

Fig. 6.22.

In social studies, we often see independent events that lead to one effect. Definitions of vocabulary words can have several independent parts that when taken together have the effect of defining the word. The key here is that events must be independent of one another.

The Writing Classroom

Once students have experience filling out the formats from written, spoken, or viewed material, they will be ready to use them to structure their own stories. Students at the primary level might want to use the simplest format. Students should be encouraged to use a variety of formats.

As a pre-writing activity, the student will find the chain format an effective structural tool that will lead them from one event to the next in an organized fashion. They may choose to start with the beginning cause or the final effect in organizing their stories.

For example, if students were assigned to write a ghost story for Halloween they might start with the first "cause" box (circled) and end up with something that starts like figure 6.23.

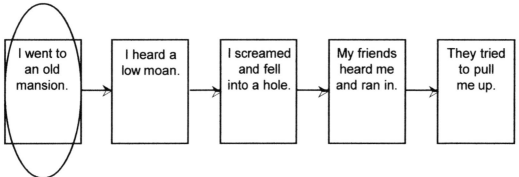

Fig. 6.23.

If students were assigned to write on a topic such as "How I Became a Millionaire," they would want to start in the final "effect" box (circled) and work backwards. Their outline might look like figure 6.24.

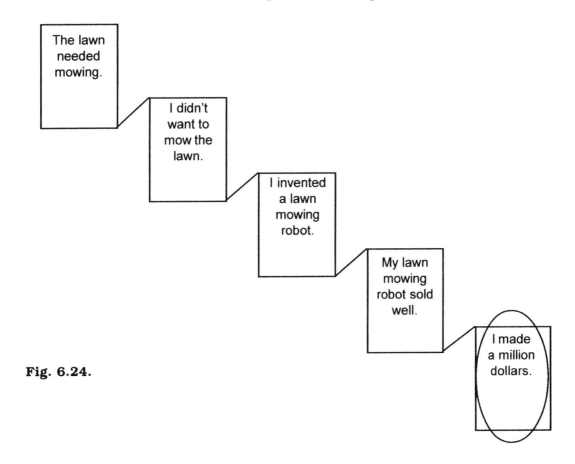

Fig. 6.24.

When using the framework as a post-writing activity, the student will be able to determine if their story has a natural flow or natural chain of events. By plotting this out together in a post-writing discussion, the teacher and student will create a visual representation of the student's strengths or weaknesses.

The cause-and-effect framework works quite well with types of writing other than narrative. The student who is taught to use the framework for a persuasive piece will find that it builds a much more powerful and logical piece. Students should be alerted to the tendency toward oversimplification in this type of writing. For example, the student might give one cause when there are many—"We lost the game because I struck out" or "Television is the reason we are such a violent country." A brainstorming session using these two statements will make the students aware of the concept of oversimplification. By listing all of the possible causes in a many causes/one effect framework, students can then decide what would be the best way to write about the topic. Should they change the wording and indicate that they are aware that this is only one possible cause or should they try to deal with all causes and indicate why this is the most influential cause?

Assessment Opportunities

Students can use any format for an outline for a writing assignment as explained in "The Writing Classroom," above. When giving points for a grade, the chart would be counted as the outline for the story. The teacher would be especially interested in seeing a natural flow from one cause to the next in the story. The topic chosen would be one that would lend itself well to this format. Using the framework during a post-writing discussion can help the teacher and the student determine where the storyline needs cohesion and what statement or statements are needed.

Students can use any format as an outline or notes for a presentation to the class or to small groups. Presenting their arguments for a topic such as: "Should we be allowed to talk during lunch time?" will lead them through a series of "if-then" statements. This will lay the groundwork for the chain rule from logic.

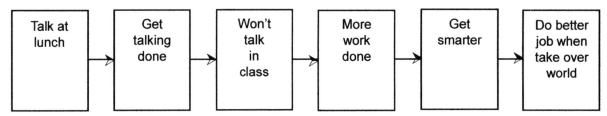

Fig. 6.25.

From an outline, illustrated in figure 6.25, the students might give the following as their presentation:

> If we are allowed to talk during lunch then we'll get all of our talking done. If we get all of our talking done then we won't talk in class. If we don't talk in class then we'll get more work done. If we get more work done then we'll be smarter. If we're smarter then we'll do a better job when we take over the world. So, if we are allowed to talk during lunch then we'll do a better job when we take over the world.

Cause and effect are regularly tested on formal reading exams. It is often necessary to add such questions to other content area tests. For example, a test might include the one cause/many effects format filled out like figure 6.26.

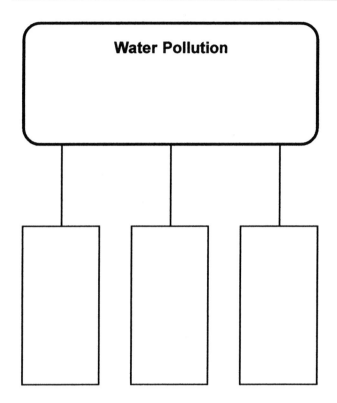

Fig 6.26.

Students would be required to write the correct effects in the boxes. An alternative test question would allow the students to look through some pictures and pick out three that showed the effects of water pollution and glue those in the boxes.

Cause/Effect Checklist

	Student	Teacher
1. Do you start with the effect every time?		
2. Can you recognize the effect when given the cause?		
3. Can you recognize when one effect has more than one cause?		
4. Can you recognize when there are many causes for one effect?		
5. Can you recognize a series of causes and effects?		
6. Can you identify a cause?		
7. Can you identify an effect?		

Effect and Cause Charts

☐	Because	☐
☐	Because	☐
☐	Because	☐

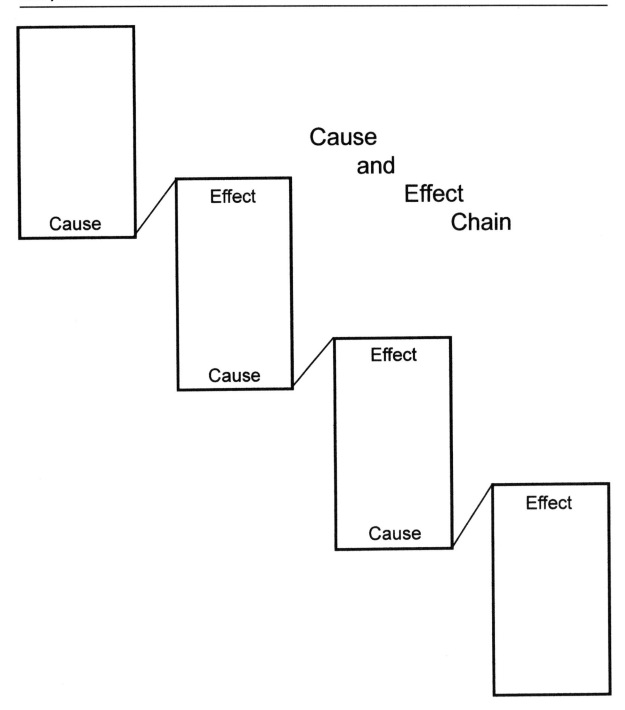

Cause
and
Effect
Chain

Cause

Effect

Cause

Effect

Cause

Effect

Cause

Cause-and-Effect Chain

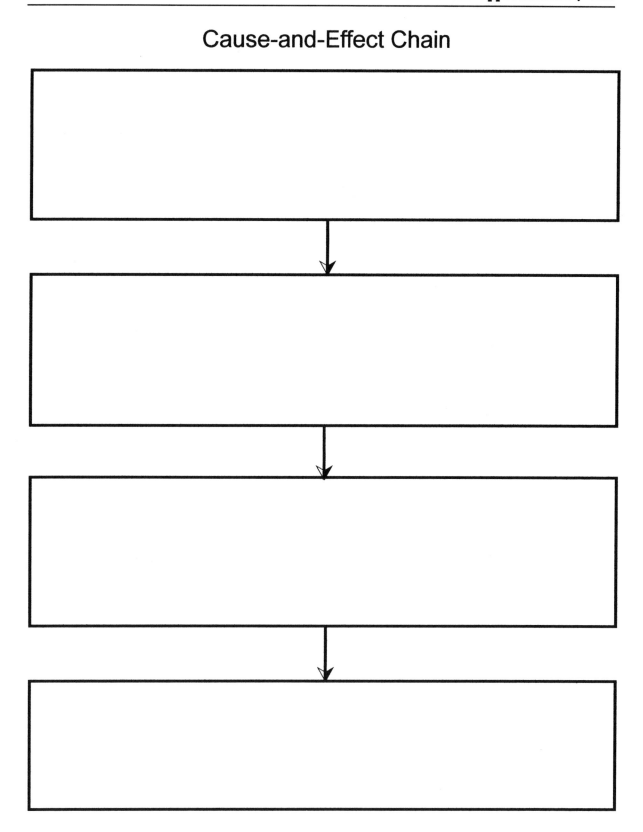

Cause

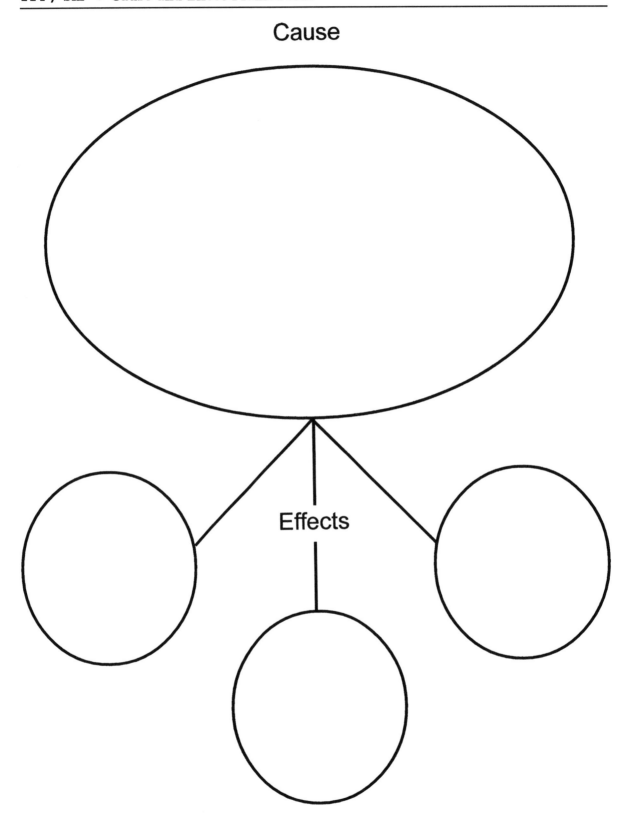

Effects

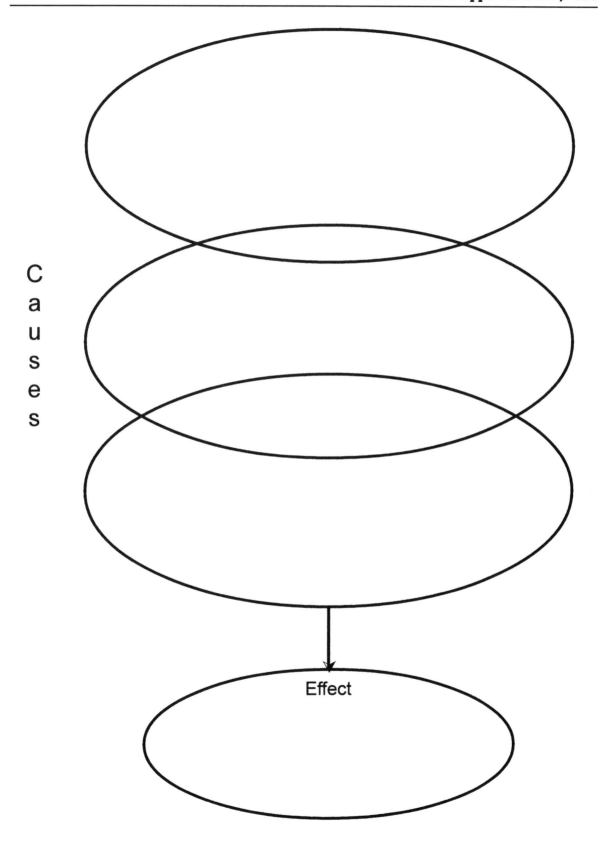

Causes

Effect

SEVEN

Classification Frameworks

WHAT ARE THEY?

Classification frameworks provide students with a visual sorting apparatus. They are appropriate when looking at the characteristics or concepts of a person, place, animal, or thing. Classification is traditionally associated with science.

WHY USE THEM?

Students will

- become acutely aware of characteristics while viewing, listening, reading, or notetaking.

- become actively involved in sorting people, places, animals, and things by their characteristics or concepts.

- develop higher-level thinking skills.

HOW TO USE THEM

Teacher models and guides:

1. The teacher chooses the appropriate framework for the class.

2. The teacher discusses how categories for the framework were chosen.

3. The class is led through brainstorming the appropriate classification for each word or concept given.

4. Items are placed on the chart appropriately.

5. Discussion is held about what information can be acquired from the framework and what processes were used in the classification exercise.

Whole-Group

The teacher or students choose the appropriate framework. The teacher or student acts as a recorder. The framework should be in the form of an overhead transparency, a large laminated poster, or a bulletin board. The teacher tells students or the class brainstorms headings to be used for the classification activity and those headings are recorded. The class brainstorms and classifies each object, concept, or person and those are recorded. Debate may occur about the appropriate classification for some items. Discussion is held about what has been learned by this activity and what thought processes were used.

Small-Group

All groups are given the same list of words, people, objects, and so on. Each group chooses a recorder. Each group determines what they consider to be appropriate headings. Each group classifies all items according to their headings. All groups come back together and share their frameworks. Discussion is held about any differences of opinion. Discussion is held about the thinking processes that occurred during this activity.

Individual

The teacher or the student decides the appropriate framework and the appropriate headings. The student sorts and records. The individual's information is brought back to the whole class and shared. Differences are discussed. Discussion is held about the thinking process that was used during this activity.

Suggestions for Use

Classification is an activity that can be done two ways. Both ways have their place in the curriculum and are of equal importance. The first way comes from the science curriculum. In this type of classification the student is given the categories and their criteria. The students are either given or must find, on their own, the items to classify. The importance of these early activities in science is that they are preparing the student for later classification of animals and plants into kingdom, phylum, class, order, family, genus, and species. At the elementary level, the teacher will only be concerned with kingdom, phylum, and class. This skill is considered basic to a scientific literate student.

Secondly, classification can be done by the student determining the categories and their criteria. These are determined by looking at the similarities and differences of a list of items given to or composed by the student. The student classifies the items according to the criteria. This extends the classification activity into higher-level thinking. There should be time allotted for both types of activities and suggestions are given in each curriculum area for both.

CLASSIFICATION BOXES

Type 1–Use figure 7.1 when items to be classified are given.

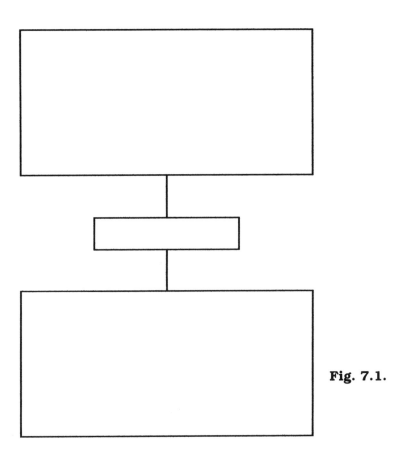

Fig. 7.1.

Type 2–Use figure 7.2 when items to be classified are not given. Classification frameworks can be used with actual objects or pictures, or by writing in the boxes.

Fig. 7.2.

The Science Classroom

Because classification is considered to be a basic science skill, the science classroom would be an ideal starting place for activities using this framework. Science is also an ideal place to use real items and allow students a hands-on approach to classification. This is also an ideal place to vary between teacher-chosen categories and student choice.

The following example is a good early-in-the-year activity to introduce classification in science. By using fewer, more, or different objects, the difficulty level can be changed and the activity becomes appropriate for all grade levels.

Suggested objects: a ball cap, mittens, a baseball glove, a sand bucket, a bottle of suntan lotion, a scarf, a sandal, sunglasses, seashell, a hotdog bun, sweater, boots, skis, picture of snow (or the real thing), and a bag of sand. (Teachers from different temperate zones might need to adjust their list accordingly.)

Students are told that they will be classifying the item as a summer item or a winter item. Rather than using a copied framework, the teacher might want summer items to go into a picnic basket or a child-size wading pool and winter items to go into a ski bag or round child's sled. These will help emphasize the summer and winter concept. One way of classifying is represented in figure 7.3.

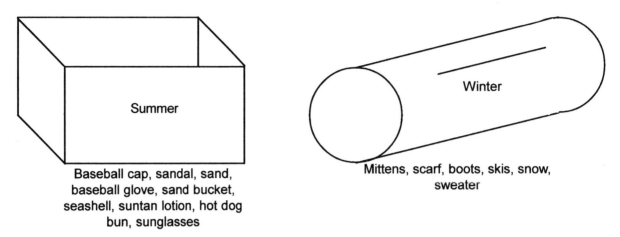

Baseball cap, sandal, sand, baseball glove, sand bucket, seashell, suntan lotion, hot dog bun, sunglasses

Mittens, scarf, boots, skis, snow, sweater

Fig. 7.3.

Some items included on the list are definitely summer or winter but others could involve some discussion. A student who skis might want to include suntan lotion in the winter group. A student from an area with cool August or July evenings might argue that the sweater is also a summer month item. Students might debate about the sand. Some would argue it represents playing on the beach and others might know it is used to provide traction on icy winter days. After the sorting is completed, if intermediate level students do not bring these issues up themselves, the teacher should ask, "Can anyone name an item that could be in either group?"

An extension activity would be to ask the students to brainstorm other ways to classify this group of items or the teacher could re-group the items and ask students to identify the categories. Some suggestions might be: clothing and non-clothing, things you wear and things you do not wear, small and large, and so on. This lets students know that classification is a very flexible skill.

Throughout the year classification centers could be set up in the classroom that would allow students to independently classify items. The objective of the center could change from time to time. At times students could be asked to formulate their own classifications. Other times the classification could be given and the items placed accordingly. The third choice would have the items in two or three groups and the student would label the classification. Individual results would be posted and a class discussion would be held about the thinking processes used. The items used in this center could correspond to any unit being taught. For example, during a unit on electricity, items could be classified as good, fair, or poor conductors of electricity. At the end of the unit, each item could be tested by placing it under the on-off switch on a circuit board and seeing whether the light comes on brightly, hesitantly, or not at all. Other center ideas could include shapes, colors, the senses, and so on. A center on animal classification might include a variety of animal stickers. Students would initially be asked to classify these animals in the traditional categories of mammals, birds, fish, mollusks, reptiles, and amphibians. Students would then be asked to create their own classification categories for the animals. To encourage an actual reclassification change the number of boxes. Possible categories can come from their natural habitat, skin coverings, food preferences, and so on.

The Reading Classroom

The center box in the second type of framework can become a word catcher. As students reread a selection, they can record words in this box. Students could then determine their own classification categories. As students read other selections they can add new words, from their reading, to the center box. Students could be asked to regroup the words they have under a new classification at any time. They can be given categories or could be allowed to choose their own categories. For example, a student who chose to classify according to numbers of syllables might have a chart that looks like figure 7.4.

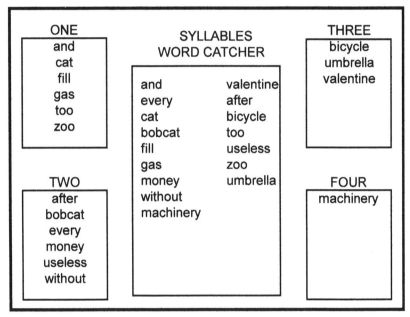

Fig. 7.4.

If teacher directed, this is an excellent activity to review phonics, parts of speech, and so on. If student directed, it allows them to see that words have many characteristics. Informal conferences can be held throughout the year and students can verbally justify their thinking about the placement of each word.

Students can classify the types of books they are reading in the framework. The student would choose the categories and these might include such diversity as: fiction, biography, nonfiction, or great, okay, poor. By allowing the student to classify the books the teacher will be able not only to keep track of the number of books but to get a sense of how students choose their books and why.

Teachers can also use classification frameworks to review characters after several class novels have been read. Students would receive a list of all major characters from several titles and be given the task to classify them by traits, roles they played, events that happened to them, and so on. This is an effective way to have students rethink and recall literature that has been read.

The Social Studies Classroom

Classifying can help clarify historical events for students. A study of the Civil War is aided by classifying the states. Students can be arranged in work groups and each group can choose their own categories. Two natural categories are slave and non-slave or seceded and did not secede. Groups should record their groupings on large sheets of poster paper and display them on the wall when complete. The follow-up discussion should make special note of where each state appears on each chart. Virginia will be slaveholding and seceded but Missouri will be slaveholding and did not secede. Misconceptions such as all slave states seceded can then be dispelled. This classifying activity can also help explain rivalries that have carried over into the twenty-first century, such as that between Missouri and Kansas.

Classifying the presidents can be an interesting activity because there are so many ways to classify them. The students could use length of time in office as in the example, or they could use party affiliation, or occupation or by what geographical locale they came from. An excellent, inexpensive, reference book to aid students in this activity is *United States Presidents, Pictures to Color, Facts to Learn* by Jean Burchfield and published by Youth Publications/Saturday Evening Post Company. By including this book in a classification center would allow students to independently choose categories and display a variety of ways to classify the presidents while familiarizing them with their names.

Figure 7.5 is an example of a classification by time in office:

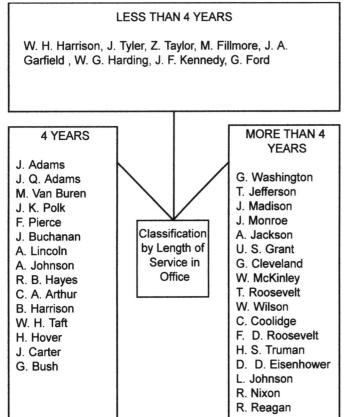

LESS THAN 4 YEARS

W. H. Harrison, J. Tyler, Z. Taylor, M. Fillmore, J. A. Garfield , W. G. Harding, J. F. Kennedy, G. Ford

4 YEARS

J. Adams
J. Q. Adams
M. Van Buren
J. K. Polk
F. Pierce
J. Buchanan
A. Lincoln
A. Johnson
R. B. Hayes
C. A. Arthur
B. Harrison
W. H. Taft
H. Hover
J. Carter
G. Bush

Classification by Length of Service in Office

MORE THAN 4 YEARS

G. Washington
T. Jefferson
J. Madison
J. Monroe
A. Jackson
U. S. Grant
G. Cleveland
W. McKinley
T. Roosevelt
W. Wilson
C. Coolidge
F. D. Roosevelt
H. S. Truman
D. D. Eisenhower
L. Johnson
R. Nixon
R. Reagan

Fig. 7.5.

During elections sorting candidates by issue, party, or level of conservatism can help familiarize the students with the issues that go into making a wise choice before entering the voting booth.

The Language Classroom

Boxes can be labeled with declarative, imperative, interrogative, and exclamatory. Three types of activities can be developed from these labels. Students can record numbers of sentences of each type during different reading assignments. (They can make tally marks within the appropriate boxes.) For example, comparing fiction to content area reading. They will discover that different types of literature contain more variety than other types.

The second activity involves recording types of sentences from their reading or writing so that the teacher can verify that they can identify the types as they occur in literature. It would be wise to set a minimum requirement. If the paper is to be graded, extra credit could be given for exceeding the minimum.

For the third activity the students are given a sentence in one of the forms and revise it as little as possible but allowing it to be classified as another type. For example, the declarative sentence was given and the framework in figure 7.6 resulted. The activity can be extended by including more sentences.

```
┌─────────────────┐      ┌─────────────────┐
│ DECLARATIVE     │      │ INTERROGATIVE   │
│                 │      │                 │
│ I am a girl.    │      │ Am I a girl?    │
└─────────────────┘      └─────────────────┘

      ┌─────────────────┐
      │ CLASSIFICATION  │
      │ BY TYPE OF      │
      │ SENTENCE        │
      └─────────────────┘

┌─────────────────┐      ┌─────────────────┐
│ IMPERATIVE      │      │ EXCLAMATORY     │      Fig. 7.6.
│                 │      │                 │
│ I am a girl!    │      │ Be a girl.      │
└─────────────────┘      └─────────────────┘
```

Notetaking

The classification framework can help teach notetaking. First determine the main concepts to be discussed and tested during the unit. When introducing the unit make students aware that these will be the areas of concentration.

Have students label their boxes with the appropriate headings. The unit studied will help determine the number of boxes needed. Four to five seems to be an average. More than that might mean the categories are too specific and fewer might mean they are too broad. As the lessons proceed, students will place appropriate facts in the correct category. Figure 7.7 is an example from a science unit that shows the labeling and some facts students have gleaned about plants from reading, lectures, and audio-visual materials.

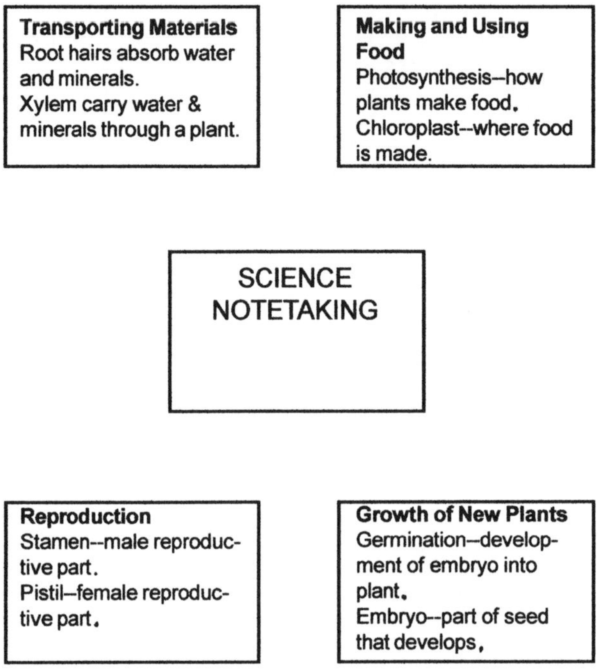

Transporting Materials
Root hairs absorb water and minerals.
Xylem carry water & minerals through a plant.

Making and Using Food
Photosynthesis—how plants make food.
Chloroplast--where food is made.

SCIENCE
NOTETAKING

Fig. 7.7.

Reproduction
Stamen--male reproductive part.
Pistil–female reproductive part.

Growth of New Plants
Germination--development of embryo into plant.
Embryo--part of seed that develops.

As a final activity for the unit, a master framework will be compiled and discussion will be held about missing or inconsistent facts. As students grow more mature in their notetaking skills this discussion can be excluded or postponed until after the assessment.

Parts of Speech Classifier

Figure 7.8 shows the shapes used. The symbols are used in two ways. The students can use the symbols to classify the words in sentences given them by the teacher. For example, the teacher gives the sentence: The brown dog went lazily to his small doghouse.

The student classifies the sentence parts by drawing the appropriate shape around each word in the sentence as in figure 7.9.

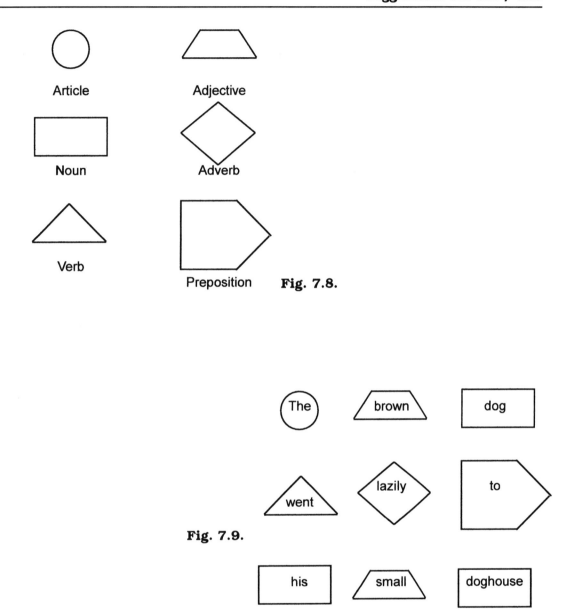

Fig. 7.8.

Fig. 7.9.

As an alternative the teacher can give the students a series of shapes and they can write a sentence whose parts correspond directly to the order given. For example, the teacher can give figure 7.10.

Students can respond with one or more sentences that meet the pattern. For example, "A large book fell slowly to the hard floor." By giving or asking for just one sentence this can be a warm-up activity. If more than one sentence is asked for or given this becomes an alternative practice sheet for an assignment.

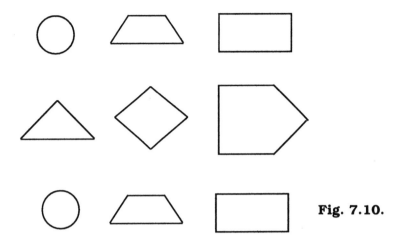

Fig. 7.10.

In a Class by Itself

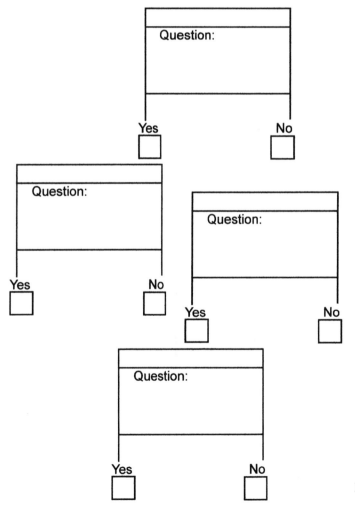

Fig. 7.11.

This framework encourages students to look at the properties of any item or concept and ask a question that can divide the field into those with that property and those without. The goal is to get each item into a classification of its own. For example, this could be used during a review of number properties (e.g., prime, composite, factors, square, roots, even, odd, and so on). The objective is to have the students come up with the question that will sort the numbers. The question must be a yes–no question and must include a number property. The example given in figure 7.12 includes only five numbers because of space limitations. By using an entire blackboard, your beginning sample space can be much larger. Each box is divided into two parts. One part contains the sample space and the second part contains the question.

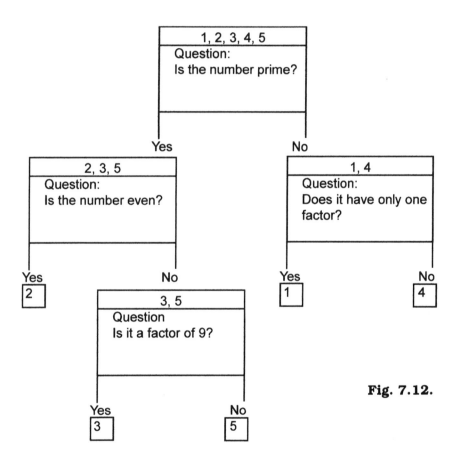

Fig. 7.12.

Students can then look back at the chart and discover what puts each number in a class by itself. The number 1 is not prime and it only has one factor. The number 2 is prime and even and so on.

This activity would work in reading with the characters from a story, in science with the characteristics of plants or animals, or in social studies when investigating any group of people or places. Resource teachers working with students who have difficulty asking appropriate questions would also find this framework beneficial.

The #!#! TV

During a math probability unit it would be interesting to classify the types of television programs available on any given night. The students would work in large or small groups and brainstorm the categories to be used and then brainstorm where each listing will be placed. (The teacher will need to provide each student with a copy of the television listing for that night. The class can decide if cable listings should be included.) Since television listings are broken into half–hour slots an indication of how many half–hour slots are allotted to each program will need to be made.

Figure 7.13 is a partial framework from students for a Monday night.

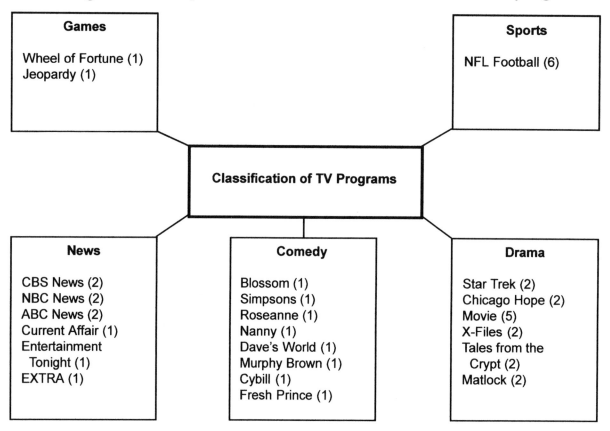

Monday Night Programs on CBS, NBC, ABC, and FOX
From 6:00——11:00
Numbers in parentheses indicate numbers of half-hour segments.

Fig. 7.13.

This list is used to answer probability questions when there is an equal chance of turning on any program listed. Questions could include: What is the probability of seeing a comedy? What is the probability of seeing a news program? What is the probability of seeing NFL football?

The formula for probability is:

$$P = \frac{\text{number of successful results}}{\text{number of possible results}}$$

Students would use the total number of half–hour segments for all shows as their number of possible results. In this case, the number would be 40. Therefore, the probability of seeing a comedy would be 8/40 or 1/5, the probability of seeing a news program is 9/40, and the probability of seeing NFL football is 6/40 or 3/20.

Students could also classify the programs that are part of their personal viewing during any week and find the probability that someone would find them viewing a particular type of program. The classification activity can also be extended into a class preference poll for type of programming preferred.

Assessment Opportunities

Classification will appear regularly on science tests. Teachers can adapt the frameworks to be used on any teacher-made or textbook classification questions. Literature offers a couple of other opportunities to do some science classification.

After a unit on the characteristics of mammals, reptiles, birds, fish, and amphibians, the teacher could read *The Bunyip of Berkeley's Creek* by Jenny Wagner to students. The first read through would be for their enjoyment but during the reread they would be asked to place the different characteristics of the bunyip in the appropriate box or boxes in order to classify this animal. This will allow the teacher to see if the student understands the characteristic using an imaginary animal. A completed answer sheet would look like figure 7.14.

After a unit on the seasons, primary students could listen to or read *The Boy Who Didn't Believe in Spring* by Lucille Clifton. As part of their assessment they could be given a four box classification sheet with the names of each season in place and be asked to draw what lets them know that that season is there. (See the rubric on page 132.) This activity is especially important in areas where the traditional signs of the season are not so obvious as was the case in the story. The teacher will receive clues as to how the student is perceiving the terms summer, winter, spring, fall. One student's ideas are pictured in figure 7.15.

Classes corresponding with a class in another climate would benefit from exchanging copies of the drawings and discussing why seasons are pictured differently.

Perhaps the most useful framework assessment is when the teacher evaluates "how" the student chooses to classify things. Are the categories concrete, creative, or off the wall? Watching and evaluating this opens a window to allow the teacher to see what connections the student is making.

Characteristics
Born in water
Moved to land
Can think
Can talk
Has webbed feet
Has feathers
Has fur
Has a tail
Carry things with their hands
Can cook

Fish

Born in water
Has a tail

Birds

Has webbed feet
Has feathers

Reptiles

Has webbed feet

Amphibians

Born in water
Moved to land

Mammals

Can think
Can talk
Has fur
Has a tail
Carry things with
 their hands
Can cook

Fig. 7.14.

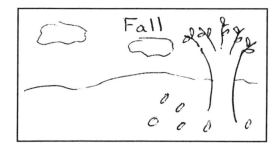

Signs of the Season

Fig. 7.15.

Name: _____

Questions (Check if answer is yes)	Self	Peer	Teacher
Are the positives I listed sound?			
Are the negatives I listed real?			
Are my arguments clear?			
Are my compromises realistic?			
Is my summary brief?			
Is my summary clear?			

Seasons Activity Rubric

4
Clear differentiation between seasons.
Many details in drawings.
Colors used are representative of the season.
Seasonal representations very good.

3
Clear differentiation between seasons.
Several details in drawings.
Lots of color but indiscriminately used.
Seasonal representations adequate.

2
Unclear differentiation between some seasons.
Just a few details in drawings.
Little color used.
Seasonal representations poor.

1
No differentation between seasons.
Very few details in drawings.
One color drawings.
Seasonal representations inappropriate.

Comments:

Classification Boxes

Classification Boxes

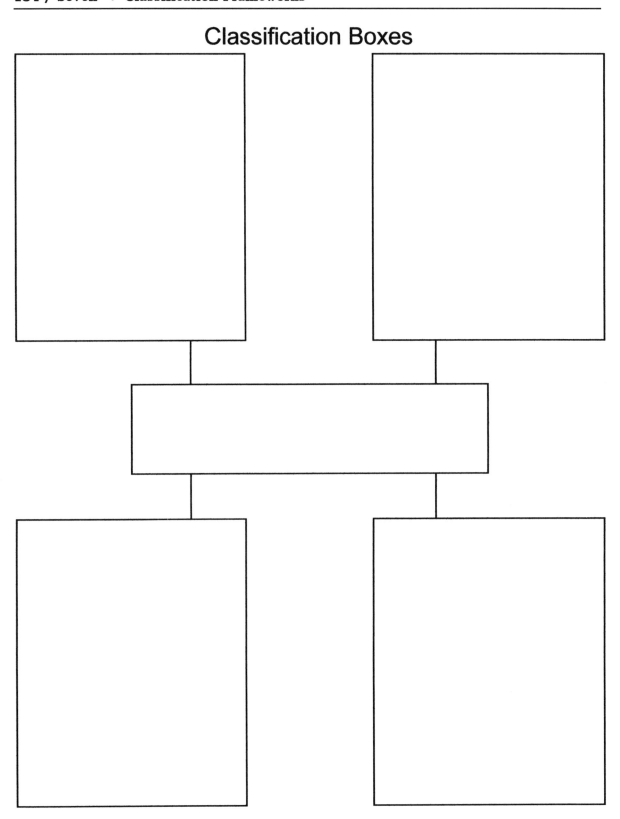

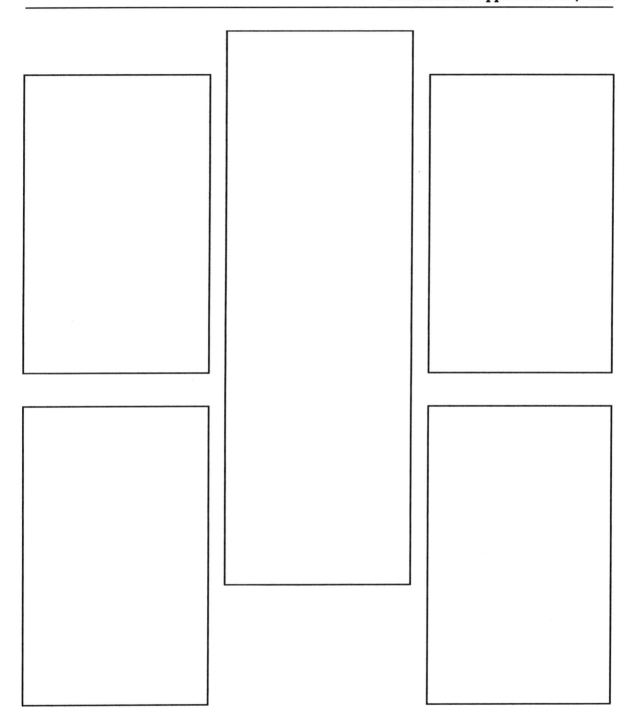

In a Class by Itself

Question:

Yes   No

Question:

Yes   No

Question:

Yes   No

Question:

Yes   No

Parts of Speech Classifier

Symbols

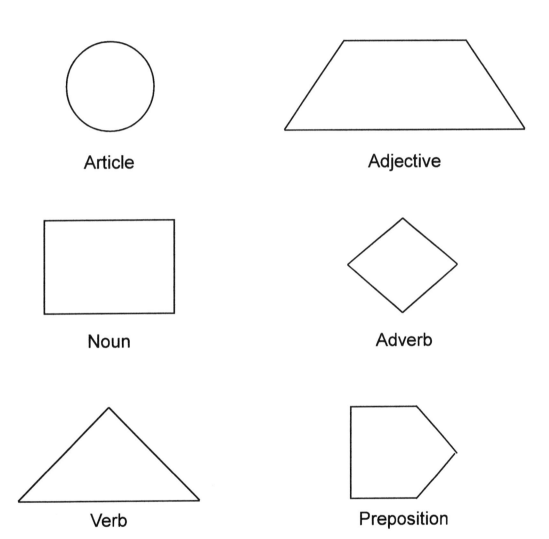

Article

Adjective

Noun

Adverb

Verb

Preposition

EIGHT

Fact/Opinion Frameworks

What Are They?

Fact/opinion frameworks provide students with a form to analyze a statement. They encourage students to look at the information and determine whether that information is supported by facts or opinions and whether opinions are based on facts or life experiences.

Why Use Them?

- Determining whether a statement is a fact or opinion is a critical thinking skill.

- If our students are to become critical readers, listeners, viewers, and consumers, they must be able to look at materials and determine facts, opinions, and viewpoints.

- When students form opinions, they should be able to support them with facts and life experiences.

How to Use Them

Teacher models and guides:

1. Establish with students that a fact is a statement that can be proved. It can be verified and universally accepted. An opinion expresses a person's belief or feeling, it cannot be proved in a way that everyone will agree upon.

2. Read aloud from an article, pamphlet, editorial, and so on.

3. List statements from the article on framework one. Look at each statement and as a group determine whether it is a fact or an opinion and why. Clearly establish that the statements listed are the major points the writer is making. This requires students to think and evaluate as they read.

4. Review with students the following information:

   • A fact is a statement that can be proven.
   • An opinion evaluates things in terms of better, worse, good, bad, and so on and cannot be proved or disproved.
   • Distinguishing between fact and opinion is important when evaluating information they read, see, or hear.

5. Have students brainstorm sources of facts and opinions—create a class list and add to it as students discover other sources. Ask students to brainstorm times when they use facts and opinions—create that list. A fun activity for a day would have students become fact and opinion searchers. They jot down statements they hear or read and decide if they are facts or opinions. At the end of the day fill out a framework as a whole group activity and have students clearly explain how they evaluated their statement. The important element is each student's explanation. Is it logical? Does he/she use common sense, past experiences, or facts when making a decision?

Whole-Group

While reading an article, story or text selection, the teacher or student should act as a scribe. Discuss the criteria for including a statement on the chart. The criteria can be set by the teacher or students. When students feel they have read a statement that belongs on the framework the scribe writes the statement down. Conversation should occur establishing why the statement is considered important. Continue to do this until the whole article has been read. After reading return to the framework and decide as a group whether each statement is a fact or an opinion and why. It is important to read the entire article before determining fact and opinion.

Small-Group

Students read an article, story, or passage and determine which statements are the major points the author is making. The recorder of the group writes the statement down on a framework; students discuss whether each statement is a fact or an opinion. They share how they arrived at their conclusion and create a statement that the group agrees with. It is important to encourage the students to listen to each member of the group before drawing their conclusion. Then all groups will come together and share their frameworks. The framework can be reproduced, made into an overhead, enlarged, or placed on chart paper.

Individual

A good way to use this as an independent activity is to give the student a framework with the statement section filled in. Assign an article, passage, story, or text to read. When the student comes across the statement he/she independently decides whether it is a fact or an opinion and state why.

Suggestions for Use

Statement	Fact	Proof	Opinion	Supported By

Framework One

Statement	Agree	Disagree	Fact	Opinion	Reason for Your Opinion

Framework Two

Fig. 8.1.

These frameworks can be used in all subject areas where students must determine whether the information they are receiving is based on facts, opinions, or both. Students must be able to view information with a critical eye and make decisions about the material using higher level thinking skills. As students read or view material they should ask themselves:

What statements are the writer/speaker making?

How has the writer/speaker organized them?

Does the writer/speaker offer support for these statements?

What is the writer's/speaker's point of view and how is it supported?

Has the writer/speaker used valid reasoning to support this point of view?

Has the writer/speaker convinced me? How/Why?

Facts and opinions appear everywhere: advertisements, editorials, newspaper articles, textbooks, trade books, television broadcasts, campaign speeches, and conversations. Each of these areas can be explored from a fact/opinion viewpoint. Either of the frameworks can apply. If we are asking students to determine whether something is a fact or an opinion, framework one will be suitable. If we want students to determine fact or opinion, plus make a personal decision as to the statement, framework two will be suitable. Following are some examples of fact/opinion frameworks.

Advertisements

As advertisements are viewed or read encourage students to isolate the claims (statements) the advertisement is making. What evidence does the advertisement use for making this claim? How do they support this evidence? Do they use facts or opinions?

Students should beware of the "either or" fallacy in advertisement: *either you buy x brand of sneakers or you will lose* and the "exaggerated claims": *x brand golf ball will go further than y brand.*

Figure 8.2 is an example of a framework completed after reading an ad from a newspaper for automobile undercoating.

Statement	Fact	Proof	Opinion	Supported By
For new and used cars	X	Go to location, talk to customers		
Protects from rust	X	Uses word "protects" not "prevents"		
Reduces road noise by 60%			X	Uses no facts or customer comments to support claim
Includes free undercarriage wash	X	Go to location and verify		
in (city) every car, van, and truck needs (product) undercoating			X	Uses word "every" - some may have it, others may not benefit from it - OVERGENERALIZATION
Only $99.95 reduced from $169.00	X	Check records to see if they ever charged that - if not - FALSE CLAIM		

Fig. 8.2.

Students looked at the advertisement and listed the statements that appeared in the advertisement. If the students thought the statement was a fact, they checked the fact box and then stated how they could prove it or what language made it believable. If students felt it could not be proved or there was not enough information or too broad language was being used, they checked the opinion box and stated why they felt it was an opinion. The intent of this exercise was to have students think critically about statements made in ads. Most advertisements make opinions sound factual. The students were encouraged to analyze each statement and to see if they could find proof if they chose to.

This same type of framework could be used when analyzing any information that is made up of facts and opinions. Students should be cognizant of words like *always, never, every, everyone,* and so on that signal an opinion. This is an important step to becoming an intelligent consumer. When students are comfortable identifying facts and opinions introduce framework two. This framework asks students to agree or disagree. Invite students to bring in advertisements and evaluate them. Challenge them to find examples of illogical statements (making claims that don't make sense), manipulation, overgeneralization, exaggerated claims, either/or fallacy or false claims.

Figure 8.3 is a framework that was completed independently after viewing a television advertisement for milk:

Statement	Agree	Disagree	Fact	Opinion	Reason for Your Decision
Milk is good for you.	X		X		Studies have been done to prove this.
Milk gives you energy.	X		X		Most foods give you energy.
Milk helps you grow.	X		X		Milk contains calcium which is necessary for bones to grow.
Drinking milk gives you a great smile.		X		X	I know people who drink milk who don't have a great smile.
Drinking milk makes you popular.		X		X	It's your personality that makes you popular.
Drinking milk makes you athletic.		X		X	It might help but you have to have talent, ambition, and other things.

Fig. 8.3.

This activity demonstrated to students how television advertising relies on visual messages as well as auditory ones. The statements were verbal statements made, plus messages that were implied through the use of actors, environment, and music. Students agreed or disagreed with these statements. This provided an excellent avenue to discuss and introduce the concept that prior knowledge and personal experience play heavily when making a decision.

It also pointed out that there are times when we agree with others' opinions based on our own experiences. It demonstrated that people form different opinions based on their own experiences. This is an important piece of information if we are to encourage students to become critical readers, writers, viewers, and consumers.

Editorials

Editorials are a wonderful source for locating and identifying facts and opinions. Copy an editorial for everyone to have or put one on an overhead. Use either framework to help students practice critical reading skills.

The framework (see figure 8.4) was completed after reading an editorial on the Religious Equality Amendment.

This activity can be done with a variety of editorials before students are asked to write their own. Students should understand that an editorial expresses an opinion about an issue or current event. The purpose of an editorial is to convince readers to agree with the writer's opinions. The use of facts to support the opinion strengthens the writer's point of view. This article used little facts to support its statements and many students disagreed with the opinions expressed. It is important to encourage students to disagree and allow them time to articulate why they don't agree. The student who completed the framework (Fig. 8.4) was questioned about statement one. He seemed to agree that this statement was true but checked it as an opinion. During the teacher/student conference he said the author did not give any data to support this statement. This lead to an excellent conversation about the importance of backing statements up with examples, research, and so on. Students should develop a better understanding of using supportive statistics when making statements.

This is an excellent activity to do with younger children as well. Recently, in a third-grade classroom, the *Weekly Reader* contained a report on a town that was making it illegal to swear in public. The statements made were listed and students decided if they agreed or disagreed. Reasons were written that both sides could accept. This clearly showed students there can be different opinions about things. The most important thing for students to realize is the need to have valid reasons for their opinions.

Ask students to select a person who has been in the news. Review newspaper and magazine articles about this person. Fill in the statement section of framework two. After exploring many articles have students agree or disagree and state why. Change the approach and list only facts. If facts were presented without emotion and without opinions would students' personal opinions change? This is an effective strategy to demonstrate how easily we can be swayed by others' emotions.

Statement	Agree	Disagree	Fact	Opinion	Reason for Your Decision
Prayer in schools is a hot button issue.	X			X	People seem to be really for it or against it. People seem to get angry with this discussion.
School children should be allowed to invite a priest, rabbi, or minister in to speak in non-cumpulsory settings.		X		X	I think school and religion should be separate.
Huge majorities of Americans support voluntary school prayer or a moment of silence.	X		X		Although the author didn't cite any survey, I think many people want morality in this country. I think that's why the Republicans got voted in this year.
A moment of silence offers respite from the chaos of school.		X		X	I don't think school is a chaotic place.
We can restore religion in our public schools without infringing on the rights of others.		X		X	I think we would infringe upon the rights of those students who are not religious or who want to keep their religion private.
We must restore religious expression to its rightful place in our national conversation and public life.		X		X	This would be against the ruling for separation of church and state.

Fig. 8.4.

THE SCIENCE CLASSROOM

The science classroom abounds with facts and opinions. Scientists often use deductive reasoning to form and test hypotheses. Deductive reasoning is using facts you know to be true to help you draw a conclusion. The conclusion will only be true if the statements on which it is based are true. Scientists also use inductive reasoning to make hypotheses. Inductive reasoning is extending what is known about a specific thing to form a general conclusion about a broader class of things. The conclusion may not be true, although using the information that is known, it is likely to be true.

The scientific process starts with an opinion called a hypothesis, meaning an educated guess. The students then use observation, comparison, analysis and evaluation to prove their hypothesis and end up with a scientific principle that is their statement of fact. In the following experiment students were presented with a pendulum (an eraser hung by string from the classroom ceiling). The teacher explained the uses of pendulums and established a base line for the speed of this particular pendulum. The speed was determined by counting the number of full swings during one minute. Full swings were determined to be the pendulum swinging out and returning to the starting side. The teacher determined the starting point of the pendulum by using a meter stick. The eraser was released to start the action. Students were asked to formulate a hypothesis about what would change the speed of the pendulum. There were four possible choices: 1) start higher, 2) use a heavier bob, 3) give it a push to start, and 4) change the length of the string. After the students brainstorm and come up with these four, they are asked to fill in their opinion or hypothesis about which will actually change the speed. The teacher can decide whether to limit them to one choice or more. The students fill in the steps of the experiment as it is taking place and finally fill in the one way that really works. Students are encouraged to write the steps as explicitly as possible since a scientist would write out how all variables were controlled (Hint: test changing the string last).

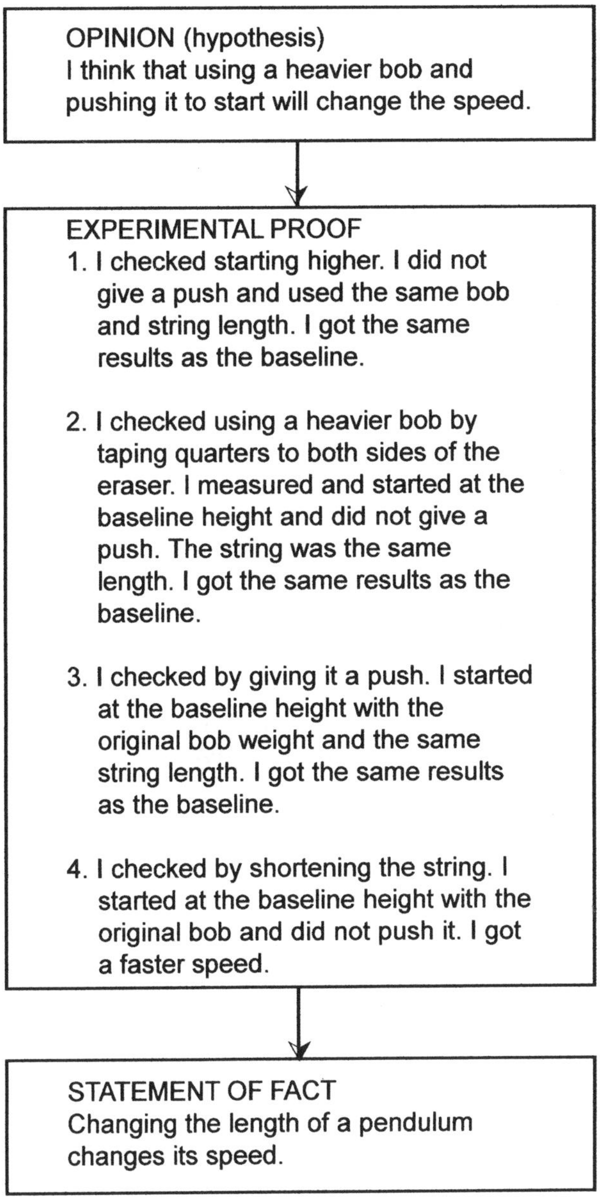

Figure 8.5 is an example of one student's sheet.

Students can also follow this same procedure in the math classroom during a decision making project.

OPINION (hypothesis)
I think that using a heavier bob and pushing it to start will change the speed.

EXPERIMENTAL PROOF
1. I checked starting higher. I did not give a push and used the same bob and string length. I got the same results as the baseline.

2. I checked using a heavier bob by taping quarters to both sides of the eraser. I measured and started at the baseline height and did not give a push. The string was the same length. I got the same results as the baseline.

3. I checked by giving it a push. I started at the baseline height with the original bob weight and the same string length. I got the same results as the baseline.

4. I checked by shortening the string. I started at the baseline height with the original bob and did not push it. I got a faster speed.

STATEMENT OF FACT
Changing the length of a pendulum changes its speed.

Fig. 8.5.

The Speaking/Writing Classroom

Your Opinion	Facts Used	Life Experiences Used

Framework Three

Fig. 8.6.

After students have explored many sources from a fact/opinion viewpoint they should be encouraged to apply their knowledge either through speaking or writing.

Advertisements:

1. Select a product or service to advertise.

2. Decide on the audience.

3. Choose a medium: television, radio, newspaper, magazine.

4. Attention getters: what will make the consumer interested: music, words, visuals.

5. Body: statements you will make—facts, opinions, support for facts, and objective of the opinions.

Framework One will provide an excellent planning sheet for an advertisement.

Editorial:

1. Choose your topic.

2. Begin with a clear statement of the issue and your opinion about it.

3. Make sure your opinions are supported by facts or life experiences.

4. Make a strong closing point, summarizing what you think about the issue.

Framework Three will provide an excellent planning sheet for an editorial.

Newspaper or magazine article:

1. Have a strong lead that attracts the reader's attention.

2. Present the basic facts and add supporting details.

3. Facts should answer the questions: who, what, where, when, why, and how.

4. Include your opinion and opinions of others.

5. Include information in order of importance in case it has to be shortened.

Framework One or Three will provide an excellent planning sheet if students list their statements or opinions in order of importance.

Persuasive Writing:

Whenever students' writing involves persuasion they will make it more convincing by using evidence to support their opinions. Evidence usually is supported through facts, examples or life experiences. Frameworks One and Three or the Persuasive Writing Planner can be effective tools for planning a persuasive paragraph. Once these are completed students can proceed:

Introduction: Introduce the main idea of your paragraph and create interest.

Body: Give reasons, facts, and opinions supported by examples, data or life experiences that support your idea.

Conclusion: Restate your main idea and encourage your reader's agreement.

Persuasive letters:

1. Determine an issue.

2. State your opinion.

3. Support your opinion with facts and examples: make sure they answer who, what, where, when, why, and how.

4. Suggest a solution.

5. Restate your opinion and ask for support.

Framework Three will provide an excellent planning sheet. Encourage students to place the type of questions they are answering in parentheses (i.e., how).

Inductive, Deductive Reasoning:

Much writing contains examples of deductive and inductive reasoning. Give students an opportunity to do both.

Deductive: have students select a book, movie, play, or television show that in their opinion was the best they had read or seen. Have them write a deductive argument to support their conclusion.

Inductive: have students select famous sayings which will be the generalizations (e.g., "the best things in life are free", "the early bird catches the worm"). Have them write two to three facts to support the quotation they have chosen.

Biased Writing:

"Don't believe everything you read."—A good adage to live by. To be objective any type of persuasive writing should present both sides of an issue. Exploring biased writing will help students make clearer judgments about what they are reading, writing, viewing, or listening to. Create a school issue (e.g., the year round school) and have students write a paragraph presenting only one side of the issue.

Assessment Opportunities

Students can be given an article to read, or material to be viewed or listened to, and asked to fill out either framework. When evaluating students as critical readers we need to ask:

Has the student clearly identified important statements the writer has made?

Does he/she logically support his/her reason for identifying the statement as a fact or an opinion?

If asked to agree or disagree with a statement is his/her decision based on logical reasoning?

Challenge students to prepare a written paragraph or a speech around an issue or current event they believe in. Tell them their presentation must contain facts and opinions. (They may want to use the Persuasive Writing Planner sheet.) When evaluating ask:

Can students identify an issue?

Can they identify and generate statements in support of the issue?

Do the facts and opinions support their statements?

Do they organize them so they seem logical?

Do they express their personal point of view?

If a personal point of view is expressed is it supported by facts or opinions that demonstrate valid reasoning?

Does the conclusion restate the issue and summarize main points made?

Does the writer ask the reader to take action?

The Holistic Scoring Guide may be used when evaluating persuasive writing pieces—students should see the guide before handing in a paper for evaluation. The persuasive writing checklist can be used in the revision stage of this assessment.

The Persuasive Writing Checklist can be used by student, peer and teacher with persuasive writing assignments. Informal writing conferences could then be held regarding the checklist.

It is important for us to note the ease with which students fill out the frameworks and where they struggle. Before any formal assessment is given, it is imperative to help students become comfortable with these frameworks.

Persuasive Writing Planner

Issue:

Facts Used:

Opinions Used:

Persuasive Writing Checklist

	Self	Peer	Teacher
Did I clearly state the issue?			
Did I make statements to support my issue?			
Did I use facts to support my statements?			
Did I use opinions to support my statements?			
Is my writing organized so it makes sense to the reader?			
Did I restate the issue in my conclusion?			
Did I sum up my main points in the conclusion?			
Did I convince the reader to take action?			
Conference Comments:			

Holistic Scoring Guide—Persuasive Writing

4	Issue is clearly identified and stated Each statement supports the issue Facts and opinions support each statement Writing is logically organized Conclusion restates issues and summarizes main points The writing convinces the reader to take action
3	Issue is stated but needs some clarification Most statements support the issue Facts and opinions support most statements Writing has good organization but could be clearer Conclusion restates issues and summarizes most of the main points The writing encourages the reader to take some action
2	Issue is implied but not clearly stated Some statements support the issue Few facts or opinions support the statements Organization is weak; it is not easy to follow Conclusion is weak; does not restate issue and/or summarize main points The writing suggests the reader take action
1	Issue is not stated or implied Statements supporting the issue are vague There is no logical support for the statements Writing is poorly organized; cannot be followed Writing does not mention the reader taking action

Comments:

Statement	Fact	Proof	Opinion	Supported By

Statement	Agree	Disagree	Fact	Opinion	Reason for Your Decision

Life Experiences Used	Facts Used	Your Opinion

NINE

Circle Frameworks

What Are They?

Circle frameworks are visual wheels that allow students to organize information into a sequential pattern or to represent common attributes or relationships among words or concepts. They encourage students to organize information around a topic or theme and empower students to look at the whole and its parts simultaneously. As a pre-writing activity they function as a visual planner for significant parts of a writing piece.

Why Use Them?

- In the reading classroom students will learn to represent their understanding of a selection in an integrated and holistic manner. They will learn to organize a selection's significant events in sequential order. This aids in their comprehension.

- In content areas, the framework provides students with a means to actively engage with the text and to organize new concepts in a way that is meaningful to them.

- Students are encouraged to analyze words, relationships, themes, and so on and recall associated words or concepts. This allows students to build bridges and discover relationships between their prior knowledge and the new knowledge they are receiving.

- As a pre-writing activity, students have a visual prompt of the parts or paragraphs that need to be developed in their writing piece.

How to Use Them

Circle frameworks can be used in many areas: vocabulary development, word analysis, parts of speech, comprehension, character analysis, problem solving, and in writing. The "how-to's" will be addressed in each of these sections. There are some basic rules to follow:

- Reinforce the concept of the clock by always starting at 12:00 and proceeding to the right.

- Correlate the framework to the concept of fractional parts or quadrants (the parts relation to the whole) by using the correct terminology (e.g., "one-fourth of the circle, upper quadrant," and so on).

- Encourage brevity.

Whole-Group

Circle frameworks work well with whole group lessons if the framework is large enough for all students to see. It is recommended that a large circle be constructed and laminated or create a permanent overhead transparency. Lines can be added as needed. The number of lines is dependent upon the activity that is being done. During a unit of study the framework can become a living bulletin board that grows throughout the unit. This provides students an opportunity to see new words and concepts for a longer period of time. When working with vocabulary, students can complete the frameworks independently or in partners in order to contribute to the class circle framework.

Small-Group

When working with small groups, a slightly larger circle than the one provided is needed. Students can draw in dividing lines as it becomes necessary. Students can be assigned different sections to work on or complete the entire framework collaboratively. When working with vocabulary, it is advisable to have students complete the framework independently before sharing with the small group. This will allow students to access their personal knowledge prior to the small-group discussion. The group can decide the categories for classification and each member or partner team can be assigned a specific category. Teams can share their responses with the entire class to help organize the class chart. The broader collection of words and the justification of classification makes the whole class share an important ending to each vocabulary lesson.

Individual

Once students are comfortable with the format, circle frameworks are a favorite with students. Students can complete it independently for evaluation, as a notetaking tool or a writing planner. Several sheets can be duplicated and put into a book format for phonics, spelling patterns, parts of speech or vocabulary work. The framework serves as a self-evaluation tool in the writing classroom. Later examples will show all of these. These activities are especially beneficial for independent work.

Suggestions for Use

Vocabulary Development

As with reading and writing, vocabulary begins with experience. Words act as organizers for our experiences. They allow us to link one experience with another. If we show students how words are related, retention, and use of those words will increase.

Circle frameworks provide an opportunity for vocabulary building. If you organize lessons around themes or units, the circle can be used to gather words that relate to the unit or theme (e.g., weather—see figure 9.1). As students read, view, listen, and participate in activities, they can search for words that should be added to the word keeper wheel. Making the circle into a bulletin board will encourage familiarity and eliminate word-repetition as you build on the framework each day. After a sufficient number of words have accumulated, the students can break into collaborative teams for a classification activity (see figure 9.1).

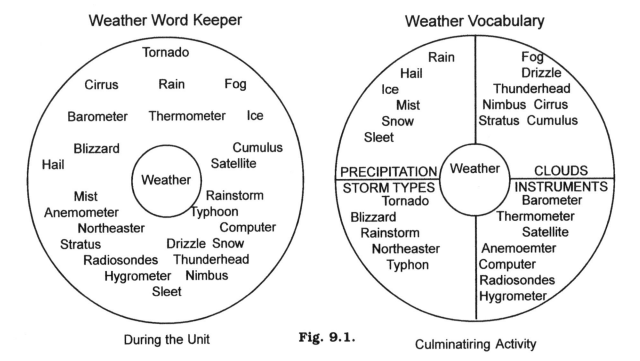

Weather Word Keeper — During the Unit

Weather Vocabulary — Culminatiring Activity

Fig. 9.1.

Each team decides four categories and collectively arranges the vocabulary words in the appropriate quadrant. This will help build understanding on how the word is used in this unit.

This activity can be done in any subject area where new vocabulary is being introduced or when students are creating associations or forming clusters around units or theme. The activity can be extended to include sentences using certain words or writing clues about the words for a word guessing game done independently, with a partner or as a small group activity. This is an excellent time to show the correlation with fractions or graphs (e.g., word clue game: "I'm thinking of a word in the top right quadrant"—partner or group guess a word; then another clue is given, and so on).

Word Analysis

Think phonics! The circle framework can be duplicated and placed into a booklet entitled "SOUNDS I KNOW BOOK." As students are introduced to new sounds they label the inner circle with that sound and add appropriate words to the circle throughout the year. Teachers could allot five minutes a day for partners to read the circle or circles of their choice. When we allow children to create and write their own lists, rather than a preprinted sheet from a publisher, it becomes more meaningful to the students. These booklets could serve as word banks when children are writing.

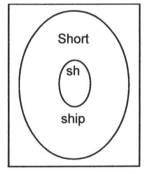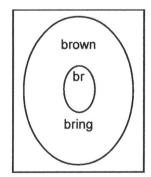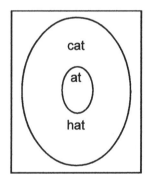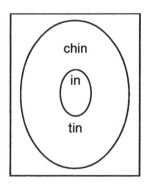

Fig. 9.2.

Older students could use this method with prefixes and suffixes. Place the prefix or suffix , plus its meaning in the center of the circle, students add base words in the outer circle that can be used with the prefix/suffix (e.g., less, without—meaning, worth, and so on).

The same technique could be used to group words by number of syllables, spelling rules, or contractions.

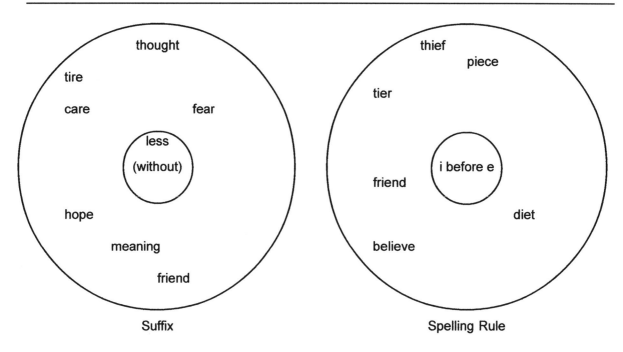

Fig. 9.3.

Parts of Speech

This framework makes an excellent recording sheet for parts of speech. Divide the circle into sections and label a part of speech in each section. As students are reading they record words on their word search paper. To encourage adequate participation, a minimum number of words should be required. Students truly demonstrate their knowledge of the parts of speech when they can identify them in the context of a piece of writing. It is even more effective when they identify them in their own writing. (They see that they do use parts of speech!) After writing a piece, they should go back and identify the kinds of words they used.

The activity can be extended by having the students complete directed sentences. (i.e., *Use your circle framework to create four sentences following this pattern:* adjective noun verb adverb. *You may add the words* a, an, *and* the.

Example: The terrified rabbit ran wildly.

Use your circle framework to create the longest sentence that you can. Your sentence must make sense.

Example: The small, timid, shaking rabbit was terrified and ran quickly, though wildly, to crawl into the old, hollowed-out log.

Figure 9.5 illustrates how the framework can be divided into types of parts of speech, such as adjectives.

Encourage students to use the parts of speech booklet when they are revising their own writing and need certain types of words. Grammar only becomes meaningful to students when they use it and recognize it in their own writing.

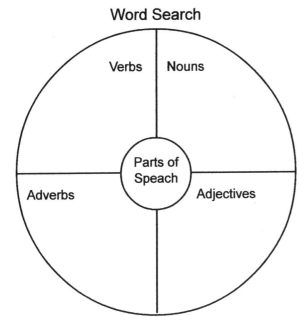

Fig. 9.4.

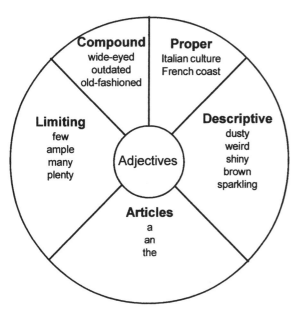

If you assemble these sheets into a parts of speech booklet, students can evalutate their own writing on a weekly basis and add words to these pages.

Fig. 9.5.

Comprehension

Circle frameworks are used to increase student's comprehension of the story before, during, or after reading.

Before

Present students with a circle framework divided into thirds. Read aloud from the middle of a story. As a group, summarize what happened in the middle section. Have students predict what happened before that section and what happened after that section. Read to confirm predictions. After reading, complete sections 1 and 3 of the framework. This works well with younger students also—have them draw a picture to tell what happened in the middle section. The students predict what might have happened before and read that section. They predict what will happen at the end and read that section. Figure 9.6 is an example from *The Indian in the Cupboard* by Lynne Reid Banks. Chapter eight was read aloud to the students. The students had a clear sense of story line and became intrigued with the events that happened before and after. This provides a strong motivation for students to read to verify their predictions. This technique has been very successful with readers at risk.

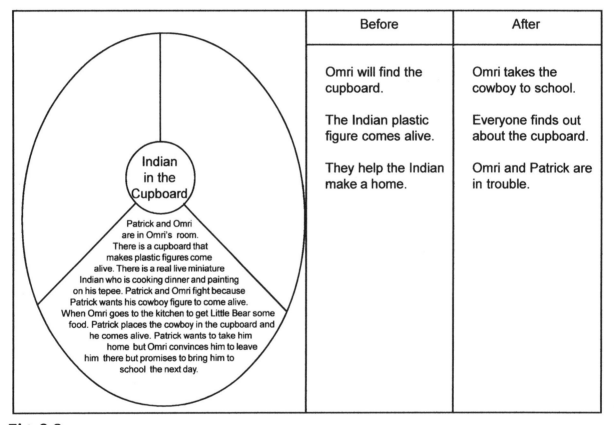

Fig. 9.6.

This activity can be varied by reading the beginning of a story or the end instead of the middle.

During

Summarizing: While a story is being read, stop periodically and ask students to summarize the events. Younger students can draw a picture, older students can write a summary statement. The student's wheel can include prompts. For example—a wheel divided into fourths could have the words *first, next, then, finally* in each quadrant. This helps students understand the logical progression or sequence of the story. Another option would provide an inner circle with numbers in it to help students when they are using the wheel independently.

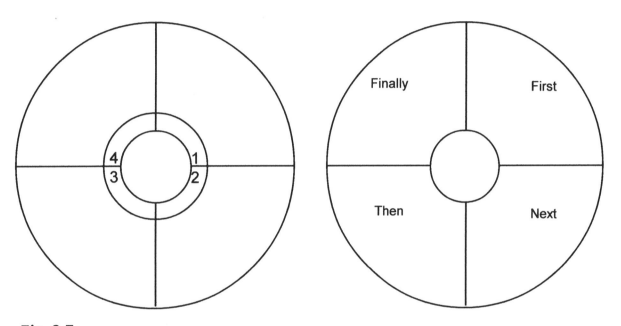

Fig. 9.7.

This activity forces students to stop and reflect about what has been read during the reading process. Students who struggle with comprehension need this encouragement to think and process while they read.

Response Wheel: The circle framework can also be used as a personal response wheel. Pages or chapters can be assigned. Students stop and record a prediction for what will happen next or tell how they are feeling as a reader. I wonder . . . statements work very well with this activity. Students begin a statement with I wonder: "I wonder what Omri will do with the cowboy?"

Question Wheel: The framework can be used as a question wheel. Prepare the wheel ahead of time with a question for each section of the wheel. Read all the questions with the students prior to the selection being read. Read the selection with students or have them read with partners or independently. Students respond to the question when they think they know the answer. This wheel works very well with nonfiction material and textbook reading. Questions should reflect the knowledge you want students to acquire. When students are comfortable with this framework, they can read the material, formulate questions of their own and exchange the wheel with a partner. The ultimate goal should be the forming of questions independently. Students have to read the information, process it, and understand it before turning it into a question. This gives them a measure of control over what they are learning and what they can learn.

Nonfiction Fact Wheels: These wheels encourage students to personalize information after a unit of study. A statement is placed in the center and students must support the statement with information they have learned (i.e., It must be hard to be president of the United States—students give explanations to show why it is hard to be president). The center of the wheel can state facts about _____ and students fill in the wheel. This is an effective method to encourage children to process information while they are reading. These pages can be duplicated to use as a learning log during a unit of study. Once students have read, viewed or listened to information regarding a topic, allow them to have five to ten minutes to write down what they have learned.

Figure 9.8 is an example of a wheel that was filled out after reading an article on sharks.

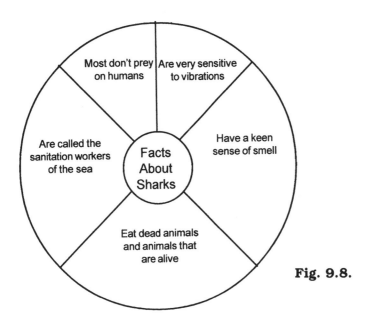

Fig. 9.8.

Notetaking Wheel: This is an excellent framework to encourage students to take notes during reading in the content area. The teacher can draw lines in with the expectation that a certain number of facts will be found, or write headings as prompts, or allow the student to record facts and draw lines after he/she writes a fact.

> Our ultimate goal: *that all students learn to recognize this pattern of organization and apply it to their notetaking and writing strategies.*

Visualization Wheel: Students' listening skills are reported to be very weak. This framework can be an effective tool to use while listening to a story. Stop reading the selection at appropriate times and have the students sketch what has happened. When the framework is complete, have them write a summary of the story using their "visualization wheel." The goal with students should be to increase the amount of listening time before asking them to sketch. This same type of activity is effective when viewing a video, movie or filmstrip. Periodically stop and have students either draw or write down what they have viewed. When viewing is completed the students can use the framework to record an entry into a learning log.

After Reading

Retell or Recall of the Selection: The framework can be used to retell the story. Either the teacher or the student divide the circle into appropriate parts and students either draw pictures or write statements to retell the story in proper sequence.

Story Analysis: When a certain emotion is shown by all characters (e.g., friendship) or a certain value is brought out in a selection, an analysis can occur using the circle framework. After reading *Roland the Minstrel Pig* by William Steig, students were asked to show what parts of the selection supported the statement: *lies can cause problems.*

Figure 9.9 is a completed wheel.

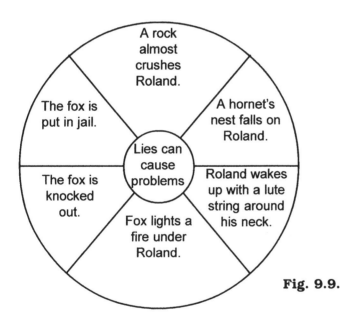

Fig. 9.9.

This type of activity encourages the students to look at a story from a certain viewpoint, theme or motif, and is often a way to encourage them to reread the selection.

Genre Study: When doing genre studies the elements of the genre can be placed in the circle segments and students can pinpoint parts of the story that exhibit this genre.

Circular Stories: Some stories begin and end in the same location. Students plot the sequence of the story to demonstrate this circular pattern.

Figure 9.10 shows examples from *The Story About Ping* by Marjorie Flack and *Call It Courage* by Armstrong Sperry. Notice the brevity. Encourage students to outline the major points of the story. Direction: Begin your framework with the location that the story begins and ends in.

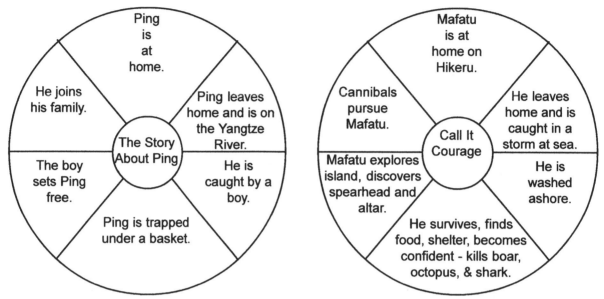

Fig. 9.10.

CHARACTER ANALYSIS

Character Traits: Place the characters name in the center of the framework and have students list character traits for the character. Expansion occurs when we ask students to list the character trait and add evidence. When first beginning to use this framework, it is helpful to supply students with either the evidence or the trait and let them supply the missing part. When reading a novel it is a good idea to have a character wheel for each character. As students progress through the novel they add traits that appear for each character. The following character study (see figure 9.11) was done on Elizabeth, one of the main characters from *The Paper Bag Princess* by Robert Munsch. A student's reasoning and thinking skills can be better understood by asking them to justify their choice of character traits either orally or written.

Character Tracing: When a character moves from setting to setting or has new encounters as the story progresses, students can be asked to "track" the character on the framework. For example, after students read *Pink and Say* by Patricia Polacco students traced what happened to Say from the moment he was wounded (see figure 9.12). This encourages students to identify important events within a story. This same activity could be used when studying historical events, famous people (the example in the second wheel) or migratory animals.

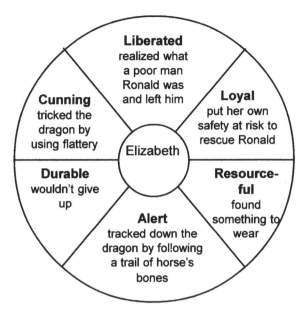

It is very helpful to have a list of character traits displayed in the classroom. Students can refer to the list when filling out the framework.

Fig. 9.11.

Examples of fictional and nonfictional character tracings:

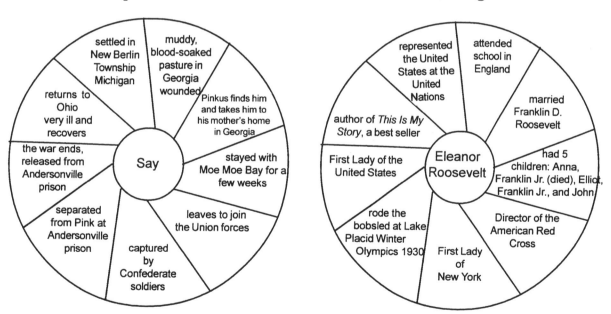

Fig. 9.12.

Character Relationships: When the character is interacting with other characters in a story the students can demonstrate the relationship by using a circle framework. The story of *Cinderella* by Peter Elwell models this well (see figure 9.13).

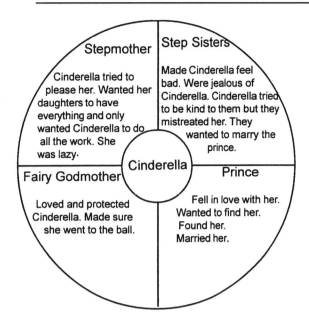

You can direct students to fill in the quadrants in a variety of ways:

show how the main character felt about the minor characters

show the interaction of the major characters with the minor characters

show how the minor characters felt about the major characters

Fig. 9.13.

In a book with more than one major character, students can complete a relationship framework for each character. A comparison can be written describing how the main characters' relationships with the minor characters were alike or how they differed.

THE WRITING CLASSROOM

The circle framework provides an excellent pre-writing planner for many types of writing.

A Paragraph

We teach students that a paragraph has four main parts:

topic

introductory statement (I'm going to tell you about . . . sentence)

detail sentences (sentences that describe, prove, support, or explain the topic)

conclusion (ends the paragraph and ties it together)

By giving the student a Paragraph Planning Wheel (see figure 9.14) we can give them an opportunity to think about what points they would like to include in their paragraph before writing.

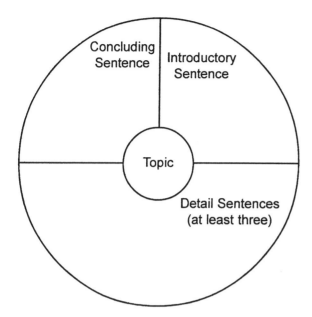

Fig. 9.14.

This framework can be adapted depending upon the writing assignment.

Descriptive Paragraph: The person or place that is being described can be placed in the center of the framework. The segments of the wheel can be divided into prompts: looks like, feels like, smells like, tastes like, sounds like *or* how it looks, where it is, how it makes you feel, and so on. When the student begins writing, each section can be turned into a paragraph.

Narrative: Students benefit from using a circle framework to plan a narrative so they can visualize the natural flow of events in their plan. They can outline the starting point, events, and ending point before writing the first draft.

Character Development: Thinking about a character before writing helps the student develop a character more fully. Students place the character's name in the middle of the circle. They think about the traits they would like the character to have and place each in a segment. They develop those traits by writing in examples of how the character will display those traits.

How-To Paragraph: Sequence is very important when writing a how-to paragraph. Students place what they are going to explain how to do in the center of the circle. The sequential steps are listed in the outer segments. This is an effective way for students to make sure that their steps are in proper order before formal writing.

Generalization Paragraph: Students are given a statement to support from their own life experiences (e.g., "life can be tough"). The generalization is placed in the center and their life experiences that support this statement are placed in the outer sections.

Poetry: The circle framework provides an excellent start for planning a poem. Students were asked to think about something that was very special to them and as a pre-writing activity they were given the planner shown below. "My Teddy Bear" was written from the poetry planner in figure 9.15.

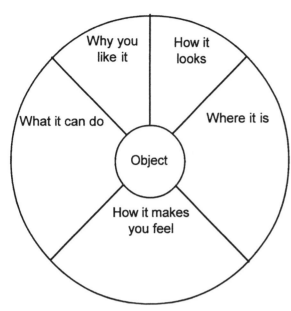

Fig. 9.15.

My Teddy Bear

My teddy bear is old and ragged
He sits on my bed all day
He makes me feel like a kid again
In a really special way

He really doesn't do too much
But I don't really care.
He makes me feel like a kid again
When I see him sitting there.

By using a pre-writing organizer before formal writing occurs, the student is given an opportunity to:

organize thoughts

spot weaknesses

view the "beginning to end" plan

Fact Statements: When you are studying a subject where you want students to have knowledge of certain facts, the fact wheel is a fun way to gather information and write a sentence about it. Figure 9.16 is a wheel from a fifth-grade classroom after completing a study about presidential elections in the United States. This can be done in any grade level in all subject areas.

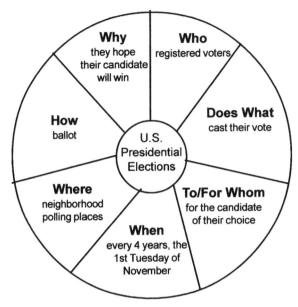

Write a fact statement about presidential elections in the United States from the information on your wheel.

Every four years on the first Tuesday of the month of November, registered voters, hoping their candidate will win, go to their neighborhood polling place to cast a ballot for their favorite presidential candidate.

Fig. 9.16.

This activity is very effective when students are initially learning to make entries in a learning log.

The Math/Science Classroom

Problem Solving: Prior to solving a problem and writing about how it was solved, students can use the framework to organize their thoughts and have a plan of action. As they attempt their plan they can fill out the remainder of the framework. When completed they can write their report about the problem from the framework. The problem: "The Goal" could be placed in the center and each quadrant labeled: "Constraints," "Options," "Attempts," "Evaluation."

Constraints: What might get in the way? What can't I do?

Options: What ways can I overcome restraints?

Attempts: What solutions will I try?

Evaluation: How well did it work? Do I have to try again?

You can extend this to math word problems by using these labels: "Questions," "Usable Facts," "Attempts," "Look Back."

Questions: Rewording of what the problem is looking for.

Usable Facts: Numbers and/or words that give you clues as to what to do.

Attempts: Working out an answer.

Look Back: What does the answer mean? Does it make sense? Was there another way to do this? What if the numbers were different?

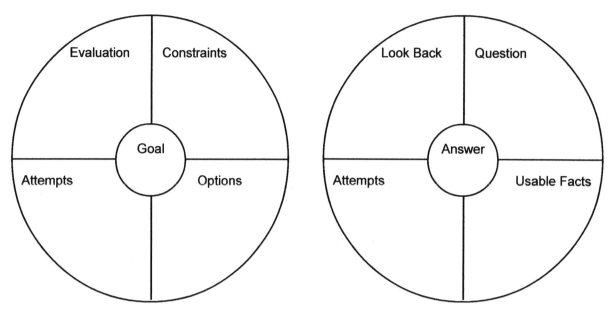

Fig. 9.17.

The circle framework can be utilized in the math classroom for fact families, vocabulary development, the teaching of quadrants on a graph, fractional parts, and pie charts.

The circle framework is perfect when studying life cycles of plants or animals in the science classroom, vocabulary development, or as a fact recorder already discussed under "During" reading activities, on page 163.

ASSESSMENT OPPORTUNITIES

All of the frameworks presented in this chapter can be used as assessment tools. When students are comfortable with how a framework is filled out and have received guided practice in filling it out, introduce it as an assessment tool. Students should clearly understand what the teacher expects when evaluating the framework for a grade. This can be done through the use of outlines, checklists, or rubrics. Some examples of assessment assignments follow.

Comprehension/Sequence Assessment

Students have the advantage of knowing what the expectations are before doing the assessment. Teachers who regularly use this type of assessment report improved scores and active student participation. It is essential with all assessment that the results be shared with the students through conferencing or class discussion. Please note that while points are taken away for errors, extra points are awarded for lack of errors. This motivates students to check their work more closely.

Comprehension/Sequence Assessment Outline

You have just finished reading _____.

Your circle framework is divided into 5 sections.

You are to recall the main events of the story.

Place one event in each section.

Each event will be worth 20 points.

Capitalization and punctuation will be evaluated: 1 point will be
deducted for each error.

1 point will be deducted for each incomplete sentence.

If no capitalization and punctuation errors occur you will be awarded 10
points.

Fig. 9.18.

Notetaking Assessment

Notetaking Assessment Outline

Read the article on sharks. As you read, record facts that are stated in
the article about sharks on your circle framework. You do not need to
use complete sentences. Be brief and state key concepts. You must
record at least 5 facts, although there are more in the article and you
will be rewarded for recording them. Grades will be determined as
follows:

Each fact will be worth 10 points.

If your facts are brief and contain key concepts 5 extra points will be
awarded.

If your framework is legible 10 additional points will be given.

Fig. 9.19.

Writing Assessment

You can use a framework as part of an assessment in writing. For example: students could take their notetaking wheel about sharks and write an informational paragraph. Have students who need to organize their paragraph before writing use the Paragraph Planning Wheel. Review the holistic scoring rubric on page 176 with students before they write their paragraph.

Problem Solving Assessment

A self-assessment checklist is also included for a Problem Solving Assessment Checklist on page 175. This is an open ended assessment where the student selects the problem, fills out a framework and then is involved in self-assessment before handing it in for evaluation. Checklists provide an opportunity to increase student's awareness of themselves as a learner.

Self-Assessment

All of the frameworks that were used as a pre-writing activity can be used as a self-assessment by students before writing the final copy of a piece. It allows the student to see if all important elements are included and gives the teacher, at conference time, a way to see if the student is judging his/her work appropriately.

Problem Solving Assessment and Student/Teacher Checklist

TASK: You have selected your problem. Use the Problem Solving Framework to clearly show the steps you took in solving the problem. Evaluate your framework by completing the checklist before you hand it in for evaluation.

	Student	Teacher
GOAL: I clearly stated what I am trying to accomplish.		
CONSTRAINTS: I listed what might get in the way. I listed the things I cannot do.		
OPTIONS: I listed the ways that I could overcome my restraints.		
ATTEMPT: After careful thought I listed the solution(s) I will try.		
EVALUATE: I stated how each attempt worked. I listed the attempts that had to be tried again. I modified the attempts that had to be tried again.		
Comments:		

Informational Paragraph

4	Has a strong introductory sentence. Includes at least 5 factual statements. Has a strong concluding sentence that ties the paragraph together. Organized in a way that facts are clearly stated and easy to understand.
3	Has a good introductory sentence. Includes at least 4 factual statements. Has a good concluding sentence that ties the paragraph together. Organized in a way that facts are apparent.
2	Has a weak introductory statement. Includes at least 3 factual statements. Concluding sentence does not tie the paragraph together. Organization is weak; facts are not apparent.
1	Does not follow paragraph format. Information is poorly organized and hard to understand.
Comments:	

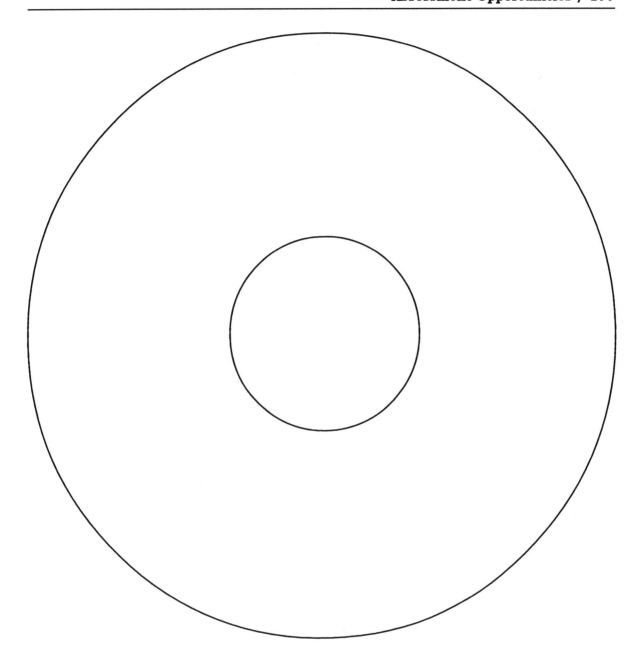

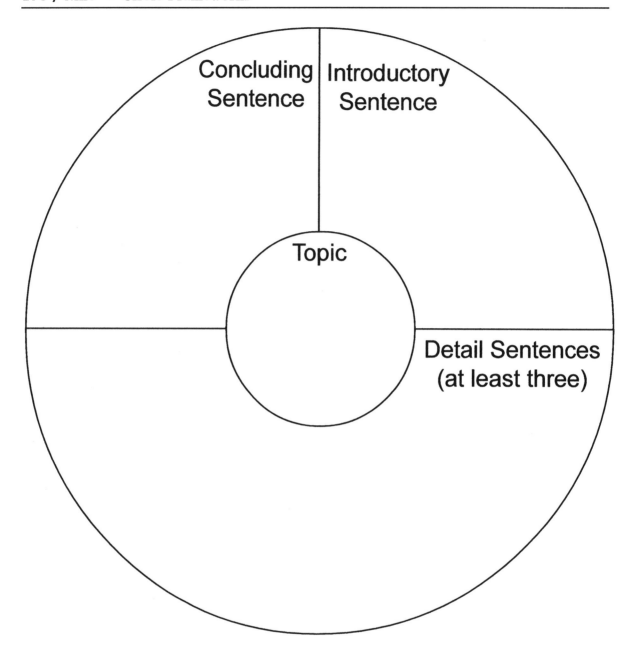

After	
Before	

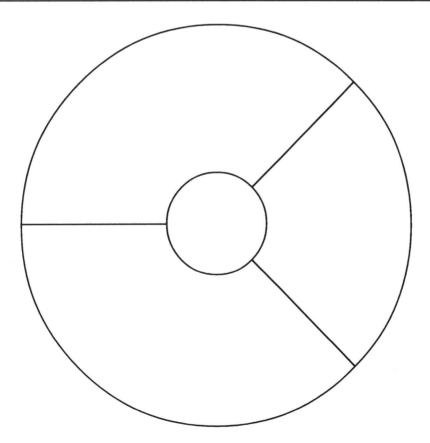

TEN

SEMANTIC FEATURE
ANALYSIS FRAMEWORKS

WHAT ARE THEY?

Semantic feature analysis frameworks use a grid design to visually represent the relationships of words and concepts within a category. They are powerful tools to use with any age student in most subject areas.

WHY USE THEM?

- Semantic feature analysis frameworks encourage students to discover the unique meaning of each word or concept and how it relates to other words or concepts.

- This framework is one of the few frameworks that displays how words and concepts are alike and different.

- The placement of words or concepts on the framework allows an easy comparison and contrast.

- Students are required to focus on the meaning of words or concepts within a given parameter.

- As students become skilled with semantic feature analysis they are asked to become more finite when establishing relationships.

- It is important for students to constantly integrate new knowledge with what they know. The semantic feature analysis framework is the perfect tool to visually represent this with students.

How to Use Them

1. Select a category. The example framework for food is a good place to start as it is a concept of which students have knowledge.

2. Introduce the framework with the characteristics (attributes or features) filled in. Illicit from students types of food. As students provide food names, move across the framework from left to right putting a + (plus) if the word or concept incorporates the attribute, or a - (minus) if it does not. (Sometimes an *X* or a checkmark is used instead of the + or -).

3. Lively debates may occur as students point out that some features do not apply as precisely to some words as to others. Allow debate and take a class vote on the decision.

4. When the framework is completed, encourage students to discuss the uniqueness of each word or concept. Discuss the meaning of synonyms as words having nearly the same meaning but not exactly; broaden this concept to include a discussion of features. While some words or concepts may share the same feature, they may not be exactly the same (e.g., potato chips and celery both crunch but not in identical ways).

5. Extending Activity: Students may choose two or three words or concepts and create Venn diagrams to further explore the similarities and differences.

Whole-Group

By using semantic feature analysis frameworks with the whole group, students will broaden their knowledge base by sharing in one another's experiences. The framework works well as a pre- and/or post-instructional tool. As a pre-instructional tool, it will help develop conceptual frameworks for students that will help them in understanding ideas when reading, viewing or listening. The teacher or the students select a topic. Words related to the topic are listed on the chalkboard, chart or overhead transparency. Features shared by some of the words and/or concepts are listed across the top of the framework. Discussion is initiated by the teacher on the similarities or differences in the listed words/concepts. Encourage students to add features, words or concepts to the framework before and after the lesson.

As a post-instructional tool, it will allow students to apply new knowledge immediately after reading, viewing, or listening, thereby reinforcing new knowledge gained. Disagreements are to be expected, and can be useful, especially when students are encouraged to defend their placement of a plus or minus. If agreement cannot be reached allow both a + (plus) and a - (minus) to be placed in the column. After additional lessons, return to the framework and see if new knowledge gained can make an agreement possible.

Small-Group

If used as a pre-instructional tool, arrange groups so each group has one or two members with a good knowledge base about the topic. If students do not have enough prior knowledge to ensure good discussion, it is best to do the semantic feature analysis framework as a post-instructional activity. Give students a framework that is partially filled out, encouraging them to add words or attributes. Each group completes a form and afterwards joins in a whole class share. Completing the framework in small groups, before the whole class share, allows students who are reticent to speak before large groups the opportunity to contribute in a smaller, more comfortable group setting.

Individual

Semantic feature analysis can be done as a pre-instructional activity (if a knowledge base exists) or a post-instructional activity by individuals. Initially, the framework can be partially filled out by the teacher. Individuals are encouraged to add to it. As students become comfortable with the framework and how it is organized, encourage them to create their own semantic feature analysis frameworks.

Suggestions for Use

Semantic feature analysis frameworks are always organized on a grid. The size of the grid will depend on the age of the student using the framework. Teachers and students will make the decision whether to use an X, a + (plus), a - (minus) or a system of range. Various examples follow demonstrating how Semantic Feature Analysis Frameworks were used. Included are different curriculum areas as well as the different recording options listed above.

Vocabulary Development: Semantic feature analysis frameworks work very well with students of all ages, even kindergartners. The following semantic framework (see figure 10.1) was laminated and posted outside the door of the kindergarten classroom. Throughout the day students were allowed to go to the chart with a partner, find their name and place a + (plus) or a - (minus) to indicate if they were or were not wearing that color. At the end of each day the whole class reviewed the colors. The plusses and minuses were erased and the framework was ready for the next day. Colors were added as they were introduced and color names were written in the appropriate color. The students loved this activity and looked forward to it. All students learned their color words by the end of the unit.

Name	Red	Green	Yellow	Blue		
Emily	+	-	+	-		
Jason	-	-	-	+		
Donsai	+	-	-	+		
Kim	+	+	+	+		

Fig. 10.1.

This same type of activity could be conducted with *objects* and *size words, the days of the week* and *weather words, objects from the classroom* and *descriptive words*. One activity incorporates Show and Tell with the Semantic Feature Analysis Framework. When students bring something in for Show and Tell the teacher writes its name on the left hand side, after the student has talked about his/her treasure, descriptive words that have been previously gathered are checked for the object. If the object suggests new words to the students, they are added to the chart. This is a wonderful vocabulary building experience. Think of the possibilities of this framework with vocabulary!

Word Analysis: When students reach the point where they are able to analyze a word and its components, semantic feature analysis frameworks are an effective tool. This could be incorporated as a weekly exercise with spelling words to aid students in remembering how to spell a word.

Spelling Words	Consonant	Vowel	Compound Word	Prefix	Suffix
Happiness	X	X			X
Afternoon	X	X	X		
Bicycle	X	X		X	

Fig. 10.2.

This chart would change as students grew in their knowledge. Once you are sure students can distinguish between a consonant and a vowel, those headings could be switched to double consonant, vowel pair, and so on. It is a good idea to leave one or two columns blank so students can add a shared feature of some of the words. The feature headings would be changed depending upon the emphasis of the spelling words of a given week and on the concepts that have been learned. Remember, while the check mark or *X* is used in this format, it could use the plus/minus.

Parts of Speech: This is a good technique to have students identify words from a text and the role they play. After reading a chapter or an article, students receive a framework with words from the passage listed. They have to reread the passage and identify what parts of speech each listed word is. The features would list the parts of speech you want to review, i.e., nouns, verbs, adverbs, adjectives, and so on. As an alternative, students can be given a framework with the parts of speech across the top. They choose words from a piece of their personal writing and complete the chart.

Phonics: This is an excellent activity to use with emergent readers as they begin to understand word parts: consonants, short—long vowels, endings, plurals, compound words, number of syllables, and so on.

Word	CVC	Short v	Long v	_____ e	Plural	
Hat	X	X				
Like			X	X		
Men	X	X			X	

Fig. 10.3.

Author Study: After reading a few books by an author the class generates a list of common attributes that typify the author's style. They are placed on the chart and as additional books are read those are listed.

Figure 10.4 is an example of a partial semantic feature analysis framework on Robert Munsch.

Robert Munsch Books	Child Is Main Character	Use of 3	"Noise" Words	Silly	Couldn't Happen
Moira's Birthday	+	-	+	+	+
Thomas' Snowsuit	+	-	-	+	+
50 Below Zero	+	+	+	+	+

Fig. 10.4.

As more books are read attributes will be added. When complete, the framework can serve as a graphic way to point out that authors often repeat styles in their writing. Encourage students to do the same thing in their writing. They often feel that each writing piece has to be brand new.

As older students become adept at semantic feature analysis frameworks, encourage them to rank their + or - with a number scale from 1 to 3—one being: "somewhat demonstrates attribute"—three being: "strongly demonstrates attribute," that is, *Moira's Birthday* used some "noise" words while *50 Below Zero* used a lot of them). We could show this by marking *Moira's Birthday* with a +1 under "noise" words and *50 Below Zero* with a +3. This encourages students to think critically about each concept and allows them to accommodate the varying degrees of inclusion or exclusion.

This same type of activity could be used with an illustrator, famous political leaders, historical figures, present day politicians, political parties, athletes, music groups, and so on.

Unit of Studies: Semantic feature analysis frameworks help students make connections during a unit of study. The following framework (see figure 10.5) was constructed during a unit on animals in the watery world. As each animal was studied it was added and the class completed the framework. Each student completed an individual framework from the class chart.

Animal	Dangerous	Friendly	Mammal	Fish	Edible	Inedible	Fresh Water	Salt Water	Fins	No Appendages
Shark	+	+	-	+	+	-	+	+	+	-
Dolphin	-	+	+	-	+	-	-	+	+	-
Eel	+	+	-		+	-		+	-	+

Fig. 10.5.

After doing several animals together—small groups can be assigned to do research on animals of their choice, add those animals to their individual charts, and then share with the whole class in a culminating activity. Remember to encourage students to continuously add features to the chart. This should be a "living" framework and grow as information is gained.

Math Concepts: Semantic feature analysis frameworks can be used throughout an entire curriculum. Figure 10.6 is an example of a framework that was used throughout the year. Every time students were introduced to a geometric figure, it was added to the chart; new attributes were added as needed. Students kept an individual copy of the framework in their math notebooks.

Geometric Figure	4 Sided	Equal Sides	90° Angle	Opposite Sides Parallel	Each Side Different Length	3 Sided	
Square	+	+	+	+	-	-	
Rhombus	+	+	-	+	-	-	
Right Triangle	-	-	+	-	+	+	

Fig. 10.6.

The Music Classroom: Semantic feature analysis frameworks are very effective in the music classroom. Features of types of songs (ballads, etc.) can be explored, composer styles, and types of instruments. Figure 10.7 is an example of a framework that grew the entire year as students learned about instruments.

Musical Instruments	String	Percussion	Wind	Brass	Low Pitched	High Pitched	Band Member	Orchestra Member
Piano	+	-	-	-	+	+	-	+
Clarinet	-	-	+	-	+	+	+	+
Oboe	-	-	+	-	+	-	-	+
Drum	-	+	-	-	-	-	-	+
Trumpet	-	-	-	+	-	+	+	+

Fig. 10.7.

This can be personalized for each class adding the number of people who play certain instruments, whether it was easy to learn to play or difficult, which instrument students had prior knowledge of, which they did not, and so on.

Genre Study: Semantic feature analysis frameworks work very well when studying the elements of a certain genre. Figure 10.8 is an example of a framework from a primary classroom. The students were introduced to several folktales. They listed the attributes that occurred in the folktales. Whenever possible, students should generate the attribute list. They formed literature circles and as each circle completed their book they filled in the class chart. When the chart was completed, each group told how their story fit or did not fit into the framework. This share time was important because students needed to use the story facts to justify their choices.

Title	Once Upon A Time	Monster	Bad Character	Good Character	Setting Changes	Magic	Happy Ending
The Gingerbread Boy	+	–	+	+	+	+	+
The 3 Billy Goats Gruff	+	+	+	+	-	-	+
The Magic Fish	+	-	+	+	+	+	-

Fig. 10.8.

This same type of activity can be used with older students who form literature circles based on a theme or motif. The unit would begin with a whole class reading of a particular title. Students could brainstorm attributes and break into their individual circles and explore how their book fit into a theme or motif. In their reading log they would record daily what attributes were shown and how. As a culminating activity each group would fill in the class chart and explain the events in the story that justified their choices. Figure 10.9 is an example framework using the theme of oppression.

Title	Small Characters	Characters Unite for a Cause	Group Has a Mission	Group Is Threatened	Characters Use Human Artifacts	Events Build to a Climax	Humans Are Portrayed Negatively
The Borrowers	+3	+1	-3	+3	+3	+3	+3
The Secret of NIMH	+3	+3	+3	+3	+3	+3	+3
Watership Down	+3	+3	+3	-1	-3	+3	-3
The Animals of Farthing Wood	+3	+3	+3	+2	-3	+1	+3

Fig. 10.9.

Please note that the students ranked their choices and this became part of the presentation. Students often find it necessary to increase the rating scale to five or ten. This should be encouraged. Following is an example from a reading log entry that was part of this assignment.

"*The Animals of Farthing Wood* really showed how careless human beings can be. It showed how urban development destroys our woodlands and the animals that live there are forced to look for new homes. It showed the effect of pesticides on the environment. It makes you see the sport of hunting as something really negative to helpless animals. We think the rating should be +3."

The same type of activity can be done in a poetry unit. The characteristics of poetry could be listed across the top (e.g., sensory images, theme, alliteration, onomatopoeia, rhyme, rhythm, visual images, repetition, and so on). As poems are introduced or groups read different poems, titles are placed on the framework and completed as a whole class or small group activity.

ASSESSMENT OPPORTUNITIES

Semantic feature analysis frameworks can be used as assessment tools in three ways. Students can receive a framework completely filled out with attributes across the top and words or concepts down the left hand side. It is their task to place the pluses and minuses in a way that will reflect the knowledge they have learned during a unit of study. The teacher evaluates the accuracy of the responses. This works best when you want students to recall specific facts. The framework on water animals or musical instruments would be good examples of this type of assessment framework. Teachers who use this type of assessment usually require students to place a plus or a minus in each box. Students can elect to add a number range.

In the second type of assessment, students receive a blank framework. Their assessment task is to list attributes and words to reflect what they have learned in the unit and then to place pluses and minuses in the appropriate box. This is a performance assessment task. Students must use self-knowledge to complete the task. The end of this chapter includes an Assessment Task Outline (page 192) a third grade class received along with their blank framework.

The outline was shared with the students and student questions were answered. An assessment of this type should only be assigned if students are comfortable with the framework. Figure 10.10 is an example of a student's framework.

Communities	Large	Small	Stores	Barns	People	Pets	Trees	Taxis	Silos	Museums	Schools	Houses	Busy Streets	Benches
City	+	+	+	-	+	+	+	+	-	+	+	+	+	+
Suburb	+	+	+	-	+	+	+	+	-	-	+	+	+	+
Village	-	+	+	+	+	+	+	-	-	-	+	+	-	+
Farm	-	+	-	+	+	+	+	-	+	-	-	+	-	-

Fig. 10.10.

The framework was presented with fourteen empty boxes across the top and six empty boxes down the left hand side. Students knew from the scoring rubric that three communities and seven distinct attributes and pluses or minuses that reflected good understanding of the community would be a C. The scoring rubric had been shared with them at several times during the unit. The students were comfortable with this assessment because the teacher had used it as a teaching tool.

The third type of assessment is a partially filled out framework. The teacher would fill out the top of the framework with attributes or characteristics *or* the left side of the framework with words or concepts. The student would have to fill in the missing part and then complete the framework.

The empty framework encourages students to recall knowledge they have learned. The partially filled out framework requires students to recall partial knowledge of a unit of study. The framework that has been completely filled in by the teacher assesses students' recall of facts. The assessment choice should be based on the teacher objective and the students' comfort level in completion of the framework.

Community Assessment Outline

1. Think about the communities we have studied.

2. List the types of communities on the left.

3. List the attributes of the communities across the top.

4. Complete the Semantic Feature Analysis with a plus or minus.

5. Think carefully and do your best!

Community Assessment Rubric

A	4 or more communities 11 or more distinct attributes + and - reflect good understanding of the communities
B	4 communities 8-10 distinct attributes + and - reflect good understanding of the communities
C	3 communities 7 distinct attributes + and - reflect good understanding of the communities
D	2 or less communities 4-6 attributes + and - reflect good understanding of the communities
See Me	responses show no understanding of communities

Food	Healthy	Unhealthy	Hard	Soft	Chewy	Crunchy	Juicy	Delicious	Moist	Dry
Celery										
Potato Chips										
Lemon										
Carrot										
Pretzel										
Peas										
Tomatoes										

ELEVEN

Flowcharts

What Are They?

Flowcharts are outlines that list, in sequence, the steps necessary to perform whatever operation is being described. Directions are listed inside certain shapes indicating certain steps in the operation. The oval indicates the start of the directions. A circle indicates when the operation is to stop. A diamond indicates that a decision is to be made. A rectangle is indicative of any of the operations that are to occur. Arrows indicate the direction of flow. After a decision box, there must be a "Yes" arrow and a "No" arrow indicating what is to be done in case of either decision. Flowcharts are traditionally used in computer programming.

Why Use Them?

Students will

- improve their organizational skills when writing, giving, or following directions.

- propose alternate endings to stories as well as a method for outlining the plot.

- check the overall look at a process or problem.

- describe the process to someone else.

- find it easier to write details.

How to Use Them

Teacher models and guides:

The teacher can effectively model a flowchart by demonstrating written directions for the students.

By using large, laminated shapes with "peel and stick" magnets on the back, these directions can be placed on the board and the shapes can be erased and written on over and over.

Always use the "start" shape at the beginning of the flow chart and the "stop" shape at the end.

Use arrows (these can be drawn with chalk) to indicate the direction of the flow.

Make students aware that no detail should be overlooked in a flowchart.

Specific example flowcharts for directions are given in the "Suggestions for Use" section.

Whole-Group

The teacher or the student draws the "start" shape. Students give steps, first agreeing on the order and the shape of box to be used. When a decision box is reached, the directions for one decision are dealt with first and then the directions for the other decision are completed. The teacher monitors progress to be sure that no details are left out and asks appropriate questions to prompt students. The teacher or student draws the "stop" shape at the end.

Small-Group

Each group should be assigned their own idea, concept, or topic. The small group follows the same directions as those used for the whole group. After completion, the small group brings the flowchart back to the whole group and shares it either orally or by placing it on exhibit.

Individual

Each individual draws their own chart, places all details in the correct shape, and uses directional arrows to indicate the direction of flow. When completed, they share their chart with the whole class, a partner, use it as an outline for a writing assignment, or hand it in for evaluation.

Suggestions for Use

Giving Directions

Students benefit greatly from seeing and reading flowcharts prior to actually writing their own. A convenient place to introduce this is when the teacher wants the students to complete several assignments independently while conferencing with small groups or individuals.

Figure 11.1 is an example of a beginning flowchart.

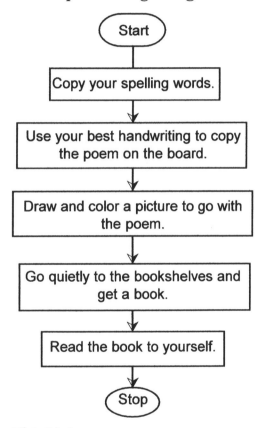

Fig. 11.1.

This straightforward format introduces students to the arrows and reading each instruction step-by-step. After students have gained confidence with flowcharts, a decision box can be added with its additional pathway.

Figure 11.2 is an example for a class with four assignments.

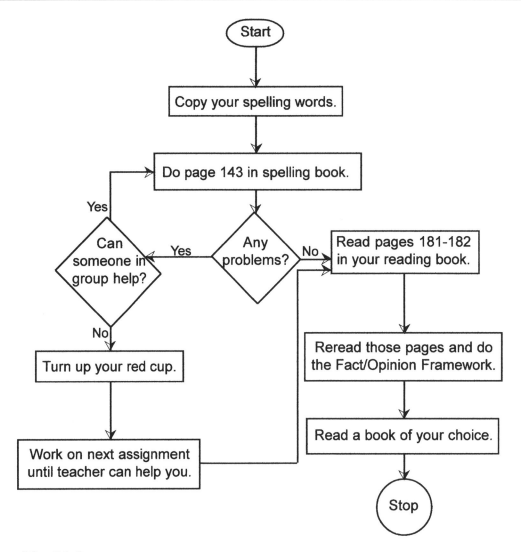

Fig. 11.2.

After gaining comfort with the flowchart, by reading and using it, students can begin to do their own flowcharts. (The red cup is a signal for help needed.)

The Writing Classroom

One of the first and simplest uses for the flowchart as a pre-writing activity is in writing directions. The assignment needs to be very concrete. Ask students to write directions for walking from the teacher's desk to their desk. Walk them through the steps by giving the directions to a familiar object in the classroom. Remind them that there will be decisions to be made along the line, and that they have to complete both routes.

Figure 11.3 is one teacher's example, for students, of directions from the teacher's desk to the blackboard: (Remind them to include all details.)

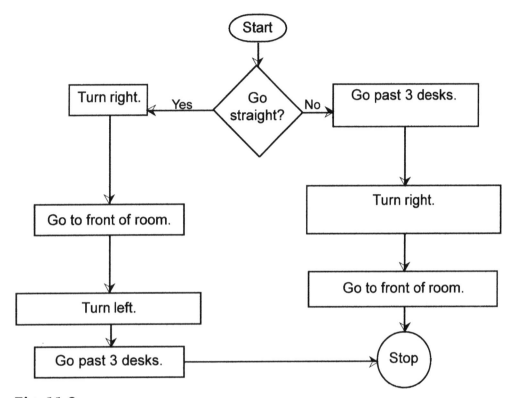

Fig. 11.3.

Students' attention should be directed to the very first decision box because they will need to include that box in writing the directions to their desk. This will encourage them to include at least two alternative paths to their desk. Some students may have other decisions along the line in plotting out their directions. Remind them to include all details through modeling.

The teacher will need to take this one step further by showing students what this would look like when transferred into writing. The teacher should have this written out on an overhead prior to the lesson to save time.

Figure 11.4 is an example of transferring a flowchart into writing. (The last paragraph is optional.)

This is an ideal outline format for any direction-writing assignment. This type of assignment focuses the student on writing in a step-by-step manner and including all details and decisions to be made. Giving directions will be useful to students in every phase of their lives. This type of assignment should be given on a regular basis.

I am going to describe how to get from my teacher's desk to the blackboard in the front of the room. After leaving the teacher's desk I have to decide to turn or to go straight. If I go straight, I would walk past three desks and then turn right. I would walk straight to the front of the room and there would be the blackboard.

If I did not go straight after leaving the teacher's desk then I would turn right. I would walk to the front of the room and turn left. I would go past three desks and there would be the blackboard.

I think the best path is to go straight after leaving the teacher's desk.

Fig. 11.4.

Flowcharts are ideal for creative writing. It is wise to model them, first doing a few as a whole-group activity, then in workgroups, and then finally individually. Students often do not realize that decisions are constantly being made during the process of writing a story. Authors often have to explore the alternative plot lines or at least discuss in their own minds which choice their character would make because of the way that character thinks. Students do not naturally delve into these "mind discussions" and often this is what makes their stories flat or their characters unnatural. When large or small groups use flowcharts, discussion about these decisions and alternative plot lines occurs. After the flowchart has been created, students can choose a plot line and write it out as their own story. Afterwards, a class discussion can be held on the difficulties of certain plot lines encountered during the writing process as well as the benefits of the framework.

Once students are comfortable with using the flowchart, individual use can begin. The teacher might decide initially to have students do the flowchart and not extend the activity into a completed story. Students can then concentrate on the plots and not worry about the mechanics of writing. Allow sufficient time for students to ponder at least two plot choices.

These flowcharts can be saved and the activity extended by having the student choose one plot line, write a rough draft, and eventually revise it into a final draft with attention to all mechanics.

The Reading Classroom

Most stories have a time when a character has to make a decision. The author chooses one path and the story outline follows. Most students do not realize that the author has to contemplate what would happen to the character on the alternative path also. Sometimes that alternative path would bring the story to an abrupt end or might lead to a confusing story that misses the author's point entirely. It would be very interesting for students to occasionally explore that alternative path and see what happens to the character. For example, in the book *Mr. Munday and the Space Creatures* by Bonnie Pryor, Mr. Munday is called upon to make several decisions. He decides to invite the space creature in, change places with the creature, push the button, and trick the Groggians. The students could change the story at any one of these points or at all of them. It will depend on how complicated a flowchart the class is capable of handling. Figure 11.5 represents a change made only at the first decision:

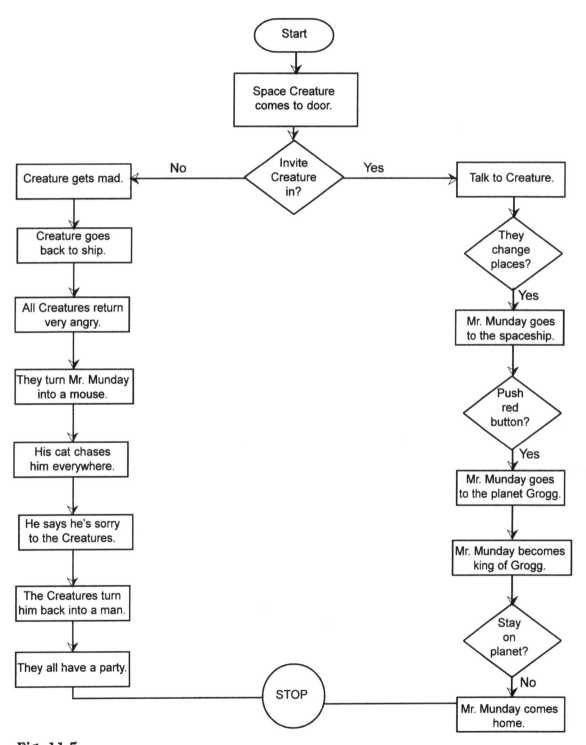

Fig. 11.5.

At this point the students have an outline of the story as well as an outline for an alternative plot. These can then be shared with a partner, the whole class, or the students could write their own story that starts where they made the plot change.

The Science Classroom

Science experiments are very adaptable to flowcharts. They always involve directions and they often involve making a decision. Figure 11.6 is from a sixth grade experiment on acids, bases, and neutrals using red and blue litmus paper. The format is adaptable to any experiment.

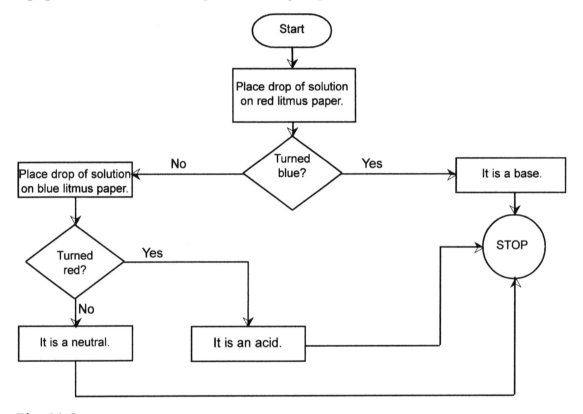

Fig. 11.6.

The Social Studies Classroom

Social studies lessons can be enhanced by presenting them either before or after reading the text in a flowchart format. Students will clearly understand the event and any decision making through this type of presentation. The teacher will want to use large shapes that have been laminated. Large, so they can be read by the students, and laminated, so the writing can be wiped off and they can be used over and over.

If the flowchart is used before the textbook reading, the teacher will need to fill in all details. As with all visual organizers, this will limit the flowcharts use in memory retention but will help the students sort out a difficult and intricate lesson where several decisions are involved. If the purpose of the flowchart is to aid memory retention as well as clarify events, then the students will need to fill in the framework themselves. For example, figure 11.7 is an example of a flowchart done after students had heard a story about Christopher Columbus. Students recalled the events. They were written on a class flowchart as well as individual flowcharts. Time was taken at each decision to discuss what would have happened if the opposite route had been taken. Similar sheets were filled out on other explorers. Students then used the sheets as study guides for the end of the chapter test.

Throughout history, political leaders and countries have made decisions that have had an effect on our present day lives. The flowchart is an excellent framework to record what happened and what "could have been."

The Physical Education Classroom

Physical education teachers work with many games where different actions are required according to the decisions made throughout the game. In baseball a walk requires a different reaction than a hit or a strikeout. The P. E. teacher can use the flowchart to teach these different reactions to the students with little or no confusion. By making large, laminated shapes with magnets on the back, the teacher can take these instructions to the playing field and attach them to the backstop or fence to provide a ready reminder to students. Instructions that require a student to stop at a base or to return to the bench could be written in red or on red paper to denote a stop in the action. Instructions that require a student to move to another base could be written in green or on green paper to denote a continuation of activity. Decision signs could be on yellow paper to note to the student that some choices and thinking are needed. Figure 11.8 represents the very beginning of a flowchart used to explain the reactions of the batter and the runner in baseball.

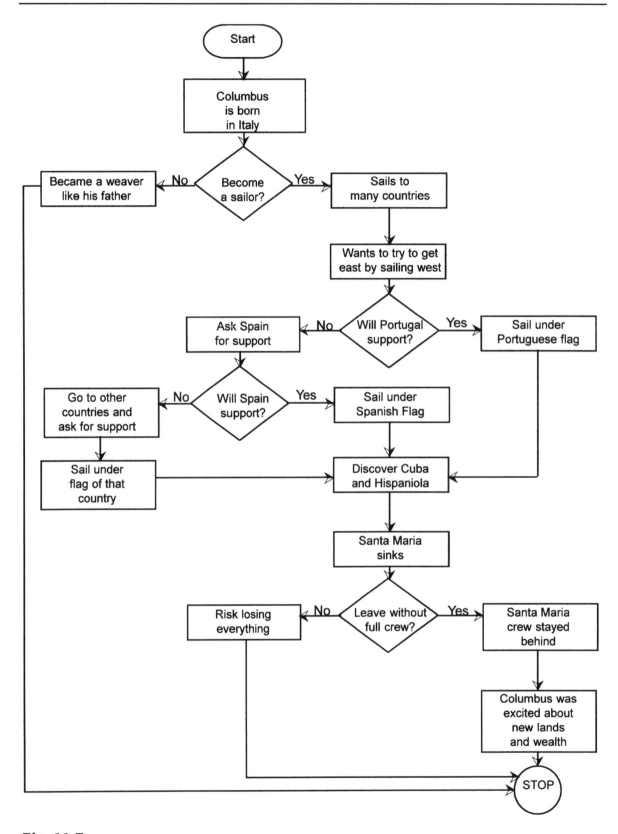

Fig. 11.7.

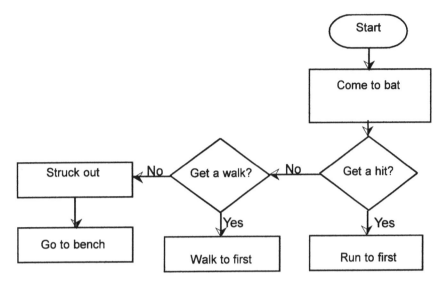

Fig. 11.8.

Assessment Opportunities

When first beginning the use of flowcharts the teacher will want to assess the student's ability to follow directions from a flowchart. Figure 11.9 is a Directions Flowchart that the teacher can use to formally assess a student's competency. This flowchart should only be used after informal observations indicate a high comfort level with the framework among all students.

The majority of the time, in science, students are given the directions and all of the steps necessary to demonstrate a concept. This is invaluable hands–on experience for the students and certainly makes the information more concrete for them. One area that has had less attention paid to it is actually asking students to design experiments themselves. These questions make ideal starting points for students to design their own experiments:

Which colors retain heat best?

Do some plants lose water faster than others?

Which toilet tissue is softest?

Which product dissolves best in water?

The flowchart provides an excellent vehicle for writing up the experiment. Remind students that whenever the experiment calls for a result, a decision box will be necessary. For example, when testing which toilet paper is softest the student will need to indicate how this ranking was made. One possible flowchart for this experiment is given in figure 11.10.

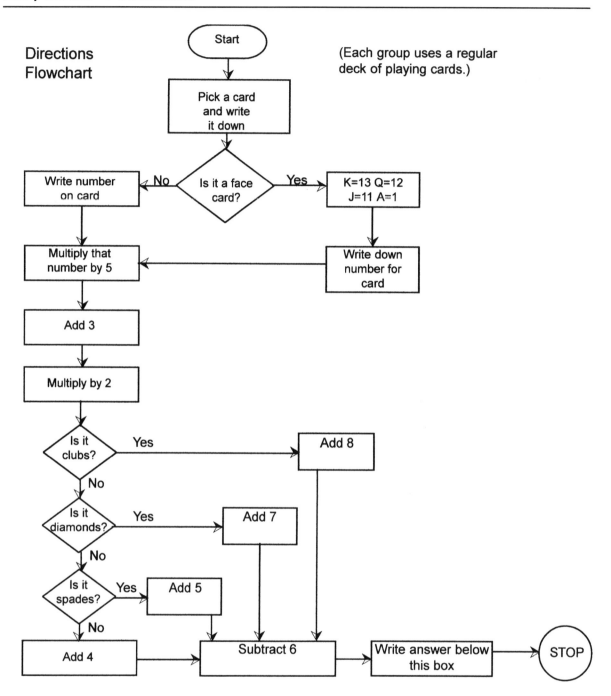

Directions
Flowchart

(Each group uses a regular deck of playing cards.)

(Number in the ten's place should be the same as the number on the card. The number in the one's place is the number of the suit.)

Fig. 11.9.

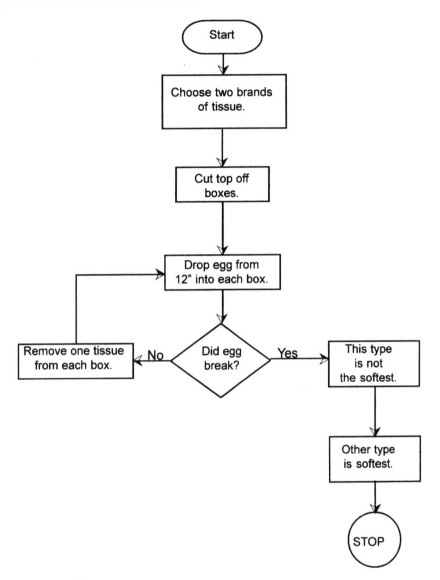

Fig. 11.10.

Flowchart Symbols

Start

Stop

Any Processing
Operation

Decision

TWELVE

Charts

What Are They?

Charts, by definition, are sheets that give information about something in the form of a diagram, graph, table, and so on. Charts are perhaps the most common form of frameworks found in classrooms. It is the intent of this chapter to present charts that are not as widely recognized as others.

Why Use Them?

- Charts of any type help students visualize information in an organized fashion.

- Charts encourage students to restructure the information they receive and record it in a manner that reflects the organization of the particular chart they are using.

- Charts model brevity and ask students to focus on key information. This provides students with a means to highlight critical information from the text and record it in an organized manner. This aids in the retention of key concepts and information.

- Many charts can serve as pre-writing planners or notetaking tools. They aid the student in recording thoughts in an organized fashion.

How to Use Them

Because charts are so diverse, the "how-to" is included with each chart presented. The charts can be enlarged and laminated for repeated use. It is very useful to have a class chart and six to eight mid-size charts for use in groups. At times, individual copies for independent work may be reproduced, or students may copy the chart into a learning log. When charts are used in a classroom, students should be involved in the construction of the chart or at least in the completion of the chart. Fully completed charts can be useful for interpretation of data, but for charts to be meaningful, students should participate in some aspect of constructing the chart. This construction or completion gives students a sense of ownership.

Whole-Group

Enlarged charts or overhead transparencies work best with whole-group instruction. The danger in using charts with the whole group is keeping all students on task. This often can be eliminated by having small groups complete the chart first or allowing individuals to have small replicas of the chart to fill out while the class chart is being completed. Jig-sawing is also effective with some charts. If the chart you are using has several "parts" to it, you can assign different parts to different groups and then assemble the chart with the entire class. If charts are used as a follow-up to a lesson, keep the session short and actively involve students.

Small-Group

Small groups provide a wonderful setting for chart use. The "two heads are better than one" rule really applies to the completion of a chart. The goal is to have students dialoguing and making decisions together. Small groups provide a good avenue to introduce the construction of charts. Many of the charts presented here can be constructed by students once they have been guided through the construction and use of the chart. By designing their own charts, students will feel a sense of ownership and become more actively involved in their use.

Individual

Once charts have been introduced and a student clearly understands how to use the chart, they can serve as individual recording, reporting, planning, or assessment tools. It is important that a student receive small-group or whole-class exposure before being asked to complete or construct a chart independently.

Suggestions for Use

Vocabulary Development

Word Exclusion Chart: This chart is used prior to the reading of a selection. The teacher places vocabulary words on the chart. Students are told the title or topic of what they will be reading. They are asked to think about each word and cross out any word they think would *not* appear in the selection. This activity allows students to make connections between words and a title, use their prior knowledge to make critical judgments, and build anticipation for the selection.

Figure 12.1 is a word exclusion chart for a story entitled *The Surprise Party* by Annabelle Prager.

Word Exclusion		The Surprise Party
aunt	birthday	lonely
telephone	tuba	desk
balloons	cars	gifts
grass	sneakers	bricks
lesson	animals	table

Fig. 12.1.

This chart involves the words that might appear in a story about a surprise party. The purpose is to have students make connections between their experiences, the words, and the title of the story. For example, a student might argue that the word *lonely* could be in the story because if the party was a surprise, the person having the birthday might feel that everyone had forgotten. In this activity there are no wrong answers as long as students can justify their choices. This activity lends itself to partners or trios working on a chart initially and then sharing their reactions with the whole class. After reading the selection, return to the chart and circle the words that did appear in the selection. Students are very eager to get into the story. This chart works well with fiction and nonfiction material as long as some prior knowledge exists.

Connections Chart: This is a very effective technique to use before or after reading, listening, or viewing. Individual students are presented with a list of words prepared by the teacher. They are asked to connect two, three, or four words that are related in some way to one another. As a whole class, students share their connections and explain why they made those connections. The teacher draws the lines between the words on a class chart. This gets messy but students love it. A method that has proved to be successful is to use different colors of markers or crayons to represent the different connections made. If used prior to a lesson, students will draw from their prior experiences to make connections. If used after a lesson, students will apply new knowledge in completing the activity. (It is best to introduce this activity by connecting two words—as students become comfortable with the activity, increase it to three, and so on.)

Figure 12.2 is an example of a connections chart that was presented to a third-grade classroom after viewing a filmstrip on Thanksgiving.

CONNECTIONS (connect three words that are related)		
Thanksgiving	celebrate	Pilgrims
feast	food	winter
Native Americans	crops	England
Mayflower	friends	harvest

Fig. 12.2.

It is the student's explanation of the connections that allows the teacher to assess how much knowledge the student has prior to a lesson or how much knowledge the student has gained after the lesson.

Word Pairs Chart: This chart works best with nonfiction material when review of key concepts and vocabulary are important. It is usually done as a follow-up to a content-area lesson. After the chart has been passed out, explain to students that they must think of the relationship between the pair of words presented and place an X in each column that is appropriate (more than one box can be marked). Students complete the chart individually, then share it with a partner. The partners must come to an agreement about where the Xs are to be placed. Partners then share the chart with a small group of eight or with the whole class. The explanation of the placement of the Xs is critical. Accept any answer that can be justified.

Figure 12.3 is a word pairs chart presented to sixth-graders after a lesson on the history of Japan.

Word Pairs Chart				
	Same	Different	Go Together	No Relation
clan/religion				
samurai/shogun				
treaty/pact				
industry/military				
samurai/knights				
conquest/surrender				
Korea/China				
Asia/Europe				
Yamato/clan				

Fig. 12.3.

With younger students you may want to start with same/different and add the last two columns when they have mastered the same/different concept.

Vocabulary Analysis Chart: Teachers place words on the chart that students will encounter in their reading. Students are given this chart prior to a lesson. It can be presented to the whole class or completed in small groups or individually. This chart encourages reflection and assessment. It also sends the message to students that we do not always know all the words prior to a learning experience but may know them afterwards. Explain to students that they should check the "know" box only if they know the pronunciation *and* the meaning of the word. After students have completed the first section and before beginning the lesson, read all the words to students (without giving meaning). Proceed with the lesson, and provide time to complete the chart. Conclude with a class discussion on pronunciation and meaning.

Figure 12.4 is a vocabulary analysis chart presented to sixth-graders before a lesson on Japan.

Word Analysis Chart				
	Before		After	
	Know	Not Sure	Know	Not Sure
clan				
shogun				
treaty				
samurai				
China				
Yamato				
Shintoism				
Buddhism				

Fig. 12.4.

This is a good pre-assessment tool for teachers. If there are many words that students do not know, instruction can take place prior to or during the lesson itself. Teaching vocabulary during a lesson, especially in the content areas, has more meaning for students because they have seen the word in print and its relationship to other words in the text.

Before, During, and After Reading

Story Chart: This chart develops good reading habits and can be used before and after a selection has been read. A large chart (see figure 12.5) is placed in view and students copy the format into their reading journal or log. The purpose is to get students to preview material, think about the selection before reading, and reflect upon the selection after reading.

BEFORE READING
TITLE: expectation: AUTHOR: KNOW   DON'T KNOW expectation: ILLUSTRATIONS: expectation:
AFTER READING
THE STORY WAS ABOUT: BEST PART: AUTHOR'S PURPOSE: THEME:

Fig. 12.5.

This chart works well with both fiction and nonfiction material. Students are asked to state what they would expect to happen, based on title, author, and illustrations. For nonfiction, the following questions should be substituted for the "After Reading" part:

The selection was about:

One thing I learned that I did not know before:

A question I have is:

Information Organizer Chart: This chart helps to develop good notetaking skills in students. Explain prior to the reading, listening, or viewing of material that they will be receiving information about each of the topics on the chart. Students complete the chart as they move *through* the material. Whole-class discussion occurs afterwards, with students sharing information from their chart. This takes practice with students, especially when listening or viewing material. Students may need to read, hear, or see the material once before notetaking, but the goal should be to have them take notes *while* they are reading, listening, or viewing the material. This works well in any subject area that requires students to locate and identify key concepts or facts.

Figure 12.6 is an example of an information organizer chart from a science lesson on the digestive system of the human body. Students were given this chart before reading the chapter in the textbook. They were not expected to use complete sentences but were expected to list key concepts under appropriate headings.

INFORMATION ORGANIZER CHART			
	STRUCTURE	FUNCTIONS	ENZYMES
Mouth	Made up of muscle, teeth, and jaw bone	Tears, cuts, grinds food	Ptyalin
Esophagus	Muscular, short tube	Pushes food and drink into stomach	None
Stomach	Large, muscular bag	Food is stored, partly digested, and churned	Pepsin
Small Intestine	Long, narrow tube	Digestion is finished, food is absorbed	Trypsin, Chymotrypsin, Amylase, Lipase
Large Intestine	Wide tube	Water and salts absorbed	None
Pancreas	Large gland	Sends pancreatic juice to small intestine	Inactive trypsin, lipase, chymotrypsin, amylase
Liver	Large, flat, soft gland	Stores nutrients	None
Gall Bladder	Membranous sac	Stores bile and releases it into small intestine	None

Fig. 12.6.

This same type of chart can be used in literature studies. Elements of a genre can be listed across the top of the chart. As students read books, they list them on the left and note where in the story each element occurred. The same activity can be done with character traits (character traits listed across the top, characters down the left—students note what the character did to exemplify that trait).

Character Analysis Chart: This chart is effective when students are asked to compare characters to each other. A trait is listed on the left side of the line and the opposite trait on the right side of the line. This produces a continuum. Each character is assigned a letter or symbol and is placed on the continuum. When completed, students can use their chart to write about the similarities and differences between characters.

```
┌─────────────────────────────────────────────────────────────────┐
│                    CHARACTER ANALYSIS CHART                       │
│                                                                   │
│  Powerful_____X_____Y_____Weak       │
│                                                                   │
│  Friendly_____Y_____X_____Unfriendly│
│                                                                   │
│  Truthful_____Y_____X_____Deceitful│
│                                                                   │
│  Ambitious____X_____Y_____Lazy          │
│                                                                   │
│                                                                   │
│  Character one = X                 Character two = Y              │
└─────────────────────────────────────────────────────────────────┘
```

Fig. 12.7.

The same type of analysis can be done with one character. This also works very well when comparing historical figures or when doing a biography unit. If you want students to justify their reasons under each continuum, leave a space for students to note their reasoning:

powerful _____ X _____ weak

reason: _____

Comparison Chart: This chart helps students identify similarities and differences between two or more things. It is useful when comparing characters, settings, authors, historical figures and events, locations, current events, and so on.

Figure 12.8 is an example of a comparison chart students were asked to complete after studying the Hittite, Assyrian, and Chaldean Empires (complete sentences were not required).

COMPARISON CHART	
SUBJECTS: Hittite, Assyrian, and Chaldean empires	
Similarities	Differences
Great military powers	Hittites helped bring the Iron Age
Used calvaries and horses	Chaldeans conquered Judah
Used iron weapons	Assyrian and Chaldean cities were centers of commerce
Ruled the Fertile Crescent	
Known for great cities	

Fig. 12.8.

This chart is an effective pre-writing planner before a paragraph comparing two or more items.

Observation Chart: This chart can be used in many areas: during a nature walk, while viewing a film, describing a place or an object. A wonderful follow-up after teaching the five senses is to have students fill out the chart for various locations in their school, home, and community (see figure 12.9).

OBSERVATION CHART	
See	
Hear	
Touch	
Smell	
Taste	

Fig. 12.9.

It's fun to have students fill this out, present it to the class, and see if the class can guess what they are describing. This also is an effective pre-writing planner for a descriptive paragraph.

Advantage/Disadvantage Chart: This chart helps students make evaluations between things. As consumers, we do this all the time. This requires analysis and evaluation. Present what we want evaluated down the left and have students think of one advantage and disadvantage of each. After a study of maps, students were asked to fill out this chart (Figure 12.10) evaluating the different ways the earth is portrayed.

MAPS OF THE EARTH		
Method	Advantages	Disadvantages
Mercator projection	Shows directions clearly, always know where N,S, E, W are	Does not show size correctly
Equal-Area projection	Shows area of land and water in correct size	Shapes of land and water are distorted
Globe	Represents the earth in its truest form	Has to be very large to read

Fig. 12.10.

Types of resources that are available for research projects could be listed, transportation methods, approaches to problem solving, communication methods, fabrics, consumer items, and so on.

The Ladder Chart: This chart can be used in many subject areas when students are asked to perform something in sequence or are asked to prioritize. It can be used as a pre-writing tool to plan a "how-to" article. When planning a newspaper article, facts that are to be presented can be listed in the order of importance from the top rung down. That way if the article has to be shortened students will be sure that their most important points are included. Persuasive articles should begin with the strongest points first—the ladder can help the student rank his/her points. Problem solving can use the ladder with the steps of the solution listed on separate rungs. When studying historical or political figures students can list their accomplishments in correct chronological order.

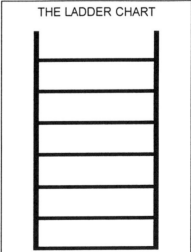

THE LADDER CHART

Fig. 12.11.

Character Chart: (Figure 12.12) This is a great chart to have laminated for use in the classroom. After reading a story, a biography or an article on an historical figure or person in the news, students write the character's name on the line above; list character traits in the space surrounding the figure, and a sentence about the character on the bottom lines.

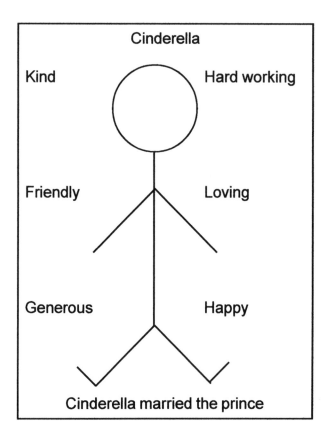

Fig. 12.12.

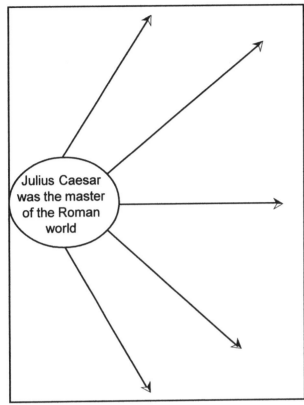

Circle Chart: This is an effective chart for notetaking. The theme or main idea of a lesson is placed in the center of the circle and notes are written on the arrows emerging from the circle. Figure 12.13 is an example of a notetaking assignment on Julius Caesar.

This is a good pre-writing planner for a "how-to" paragraph. The how-to can be placed in the circle and the steps to follow on the arrows.

Prediction Charts: Using prediction charts with nonfiction material is a good way to help children build conceptual backgrounds before reading, viewing or listening, especially in the content areas. Figure 12.14 is an example of a prediction chart used with a second grade class before reading material on ladybugs. Students really enjoy this activity. This is an excellent way for a teacher to highlight material that is essential for students to key into.

Fig. 12.13.

	LADYBUG PREDICTION CHART	
Before Reading		After Reading
Y N	A male ladybug knows a female by her smell.	Y N
Y N	The ladybug's eggs are bright red.	Y N
Y N	Larva start looking for food right away.	Y N
Y N	The larvae has eight legs.	Y N
Y N	The pupa is soft and orange.	Y N
Y N	The adult ladybug comes out of the pupa at night.	Y N
Y N	The adult ladybug's wind cases are soft.	Y N
Y N	Ladybugs fly very fast.	Y N
Y N	The ladybug sleeps all winter long.	Y N

Fig. 12.14.

Five-Star Question: This chart is great to laminate or run off for students. Familiarize students with the 4 or 5 star rating system for hotels and restaurants. Explain a five star question has to be their best. Either in teams or as individuals, students create their "best" question about material that has just been studied. The teacher then places the questions on the star, (Figure 12.15) one question for each point. The next day, or later the same day, the students read their questions to the class and the class answers them. When students are comfortable with formulating their own questions, they can complete their own 5 star questionnaire and exchange it with a partner. When students are asked to formulate their own questions, they are encouraged to *absorb, process* and *rephrase* information they have received.

Fig. 12.15.

A System and Its Parts Chart: This chart is effective when we want students to understand the concept of a system. A system is a group of things or parts working together to form a whole. This chart should be presented and modeled carefully before we expect teams or individuals to complete it. The wagon chart (Figure 12.16) is an example of an introductory lesson demonstrating "how-to" use the chart.

This form could be used in science units, government studies, to explain a school system, a family, etc. It helps the students focus on the parts while keeping the whole in mind.

A SYSTEM AND ITS PARTS			
SYSTEM	PARTS	FUNCTION OF EACH PART	HOW THEY WORK AS A WHOLE
Wagon	Wheel	Makes it move	The handle allows someone to push or pull the wagon. When they do, the axles allow the wheels to turn, which makes the wagon move. The frame keeps it together.
	Axle	Allows wheels to turn	
	Bed	Provides space for objects	
	Handle	Allows it to be pulled	
	Frame	Holds it all together	

Fig. 12.16.

Description/Topic Chart: This chart is useful when doing expository text units in the content areas. The topic that is being explored is placed in the center. The students can complete the chart as a whole class or break into groups and define the topic as it applies to the various sub-groups. Figure 12.17 is a chart that was created when studying the events leading to World War II. This can be done as a whole group activity. The class would read or view information on Germany. The information would be summarized and placed on the chart. A technique that aids in covering more material in a shorter length of time breaks students into collaborative groups and assigns each group a country. The group is responsible for gathering the necessary information for the chart and then presenting it to the entire class. The responsibility for teaching the information lies with each group—they become the "experts" for their country.

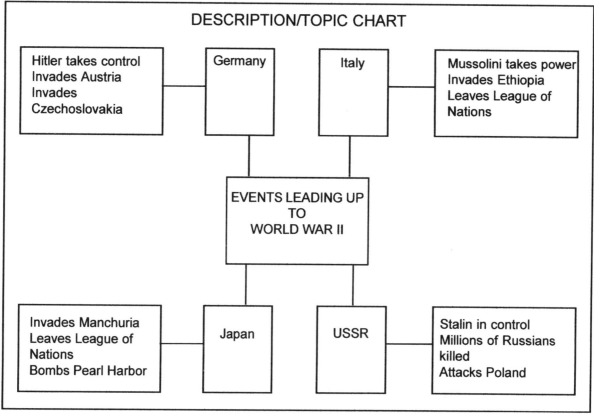

Fig. 12.17.

ASSESSMENT OPPORTUNITIES

Most of the charts presented could be used as assessment tools. Each should be accompanied with an assessment outline, checklist or rubric so students have a clear understanding of what will be evaluated. At times a completed chart could be given to the students with an assessment task designed to use the information from the chart. Some chart assessment might be extended through a writing activity that will allow the student to explain choices or extend a listing into a paragraph. Three assessment tasks follow to demonstrate this.

Assessment Task 1: This is the chart (figure 12.18) the class completed on the digestive system. Use the information on this chart to give a clear explanation of the digestive system and how it works. Pretend you are a piece of food and tell what is happening to you from the time you enter the mouth until you reach the large intestine. When complete, use the Assessment Checklist to evaluate your writing.

INFORMATION ORGANIZER CHART			
	STRUCTURE	FUNCTIONS	ENZYMES
Mouth	Made up of muscle, teeth, and jaw bone	Tears, cuts, grinds food	Ptyalin
Esophagus	Muscular, short tube	Pushes food and drink into stomach	None
Stomach	Large, muscular bag	Food is stored, partly digested, and churned	Pepsin
Small Intestine	Long, narrow tube	Digestion is finished, food is absorbed	Trypsin, Chymotrypsin, Amylase, Lipase
Large Intestine	Wide tube	Water and salts absorbed	None
Pancreas	Large gland	Sends pancreatic juice to small intestine	Inactive trypsin, lipase, chymotrypsin, amylase
Liver	Large, flat, soft gland	Stores nutrients	None
Gall Bladder	Membranous sac	Stores bile and releases it into small intestine	None

Fig. 12.18.

Student checklist and rubric follow assessment pages.

ASSESSMENT TASK: Connect three words that are related. At the bottom of the chart tell what words you connected and how they are related.

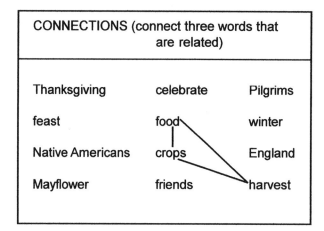

I connected food, crops, and harvest. The Pilgrims planted crops. Then they had to harvest the crops so they would have food to eat.

Fig. 12.19.

The **Character Chart** could be used to assess a student's ability to determine character traits if we ask them to support their answers with a brief example from the story that supports the specific trait. It is also a good idea to have a minimum number of character traits that will be accepted. This is an ideal assessment after studying a famous historical or contemporary figure.

Assessment Task 2: Choose one of the dictators we have been studying. Complete the character chart on that dictator. You must list at least 5 character traits. Write a brief paragraph in the space below the chart to explain why you chose the character traits for your dictator.

Figure 12.20 was completed by a sixth grade student as an assessment task.

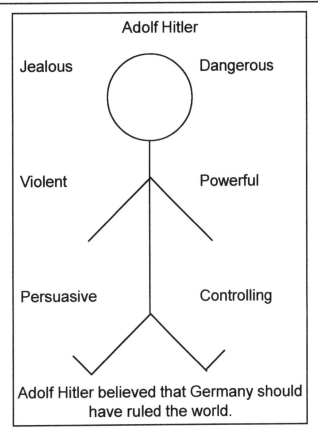

Adolf Hitler was a very jealous man. When he lived in Vienna he was very jealous of the successful Jewish professionals. He was a very dangerous man. He was the supreme ruler of Germany and used his power in violent ways. He had a way of speaking that led the German people to believe in what he was saying. He was very persuasive and could control them. He set up concentration camps where millions of Jews were killed and tortured. This showed what a violent man he was.

Fig. 12.20.

Other suggestions for assessment follow:

The **Information Organizer Chart, Circle Chart and Description/Topic Chart** provide a good assessment of notetaking skills. Make sure students understand that they are being evaluated on their ability to identify key concepts that support the topic and their ability to reword information in a manner that is brief yet informative. These can be used with information that is read, viewed or listened to.

The **Comparison Chart** is a good assessment of a student's ability to identify similarities and differences. This is an excellent chart to extend to a writing assignment. The student may fill in the chart and then write a paragraph describing similarities and differences between the topics or be given a chart that has already been completed and asked to write a paragraph from the information on the chart.

A System and Its Parts Chart provides a good assessment tool when evaluating a student's ability to break a system into its parts, define each part and the role it plays as part of the whole. We could take the digestive system Information Organizer Chart and ask students to complete the System and Its Parts Chart for the digestive system. That encourages students to take information that is organized in one way and reorganize that information in another manner. If students can do this, it will demonstrate complete understanding of the topic.

The Advantage/Disadvantage Chart would be an excellent assessment of a student's ability to receive information about a topic and evaluate it. A fun activity to do with this chart is giving the student three travel brochures describing three different types of vacation packages. After reading the brochures they have to list an advantage and disadvantage for each plan.

Student Checklist for Digestive System Assessment		
	Student	Teacher
I chose a piece of food and explained what happened to it.		
I included all 8 parts of the digestive system.		
I explained the function of each part.		
I told what happened to the piece of food in the correct order.		
I used the information on the chart to give a clear explanation of what happens to a piece of food when digesting.		
I used the information on the chart to explain the roles of the pancreas, liver, and gall bladder.		
After reading my paper and reading the Scoring Rubric I think my grade will be _____.		
Comments:		

Digestive System Assessment Scoring Rubric

4	Explained the digestive system as a piece of food on a digestive journey. All 8 parts of the digestive system were included. The digestive system was explained sequentially. A clear, detailed explanation of each part and its function was included. Necessary information from the chart was included. Grammar and mechanical errors did not interfere with meaning.
3	Explained the digestive system as a piece of food on a digestive journey. All 8 parts of the digestive system were included. The digestive system was explained sequentially. A good explanation of each part and its function was included, with some detail. Necessary information from the chart was included. Grammar and mechanical errors did not interfere with meaning.
2	Explained the digestive system as a piece of food on a digestive journey. All 8 parts of the digestive system were included. The digestive system was explained sequentially. A satisfactory explanation of each part and its function was included, with little detail added. Some but not all necessary information from the chart was included. Grammar and mechanical errors did not interfere with meaning.
1	Explained the digestive system as a piece of food on a digestive journey. All 8 parts of the digestive system were included. The digestive system was not explained sequentially. An explanation of each part and its function, was included, but little detail added. Little or no information from the chart was included. Grammar and mechanical errors did interfere with meaning.

Final Thoughts

Throughout this book, certain methods have been emphasized. These methods have special significance for the successful use of visual organizers. In closing, we wish to reiterate these methods as well as provide further information to ensure success.

Model It

The key to successful independent or small-group use of the frameworks is in the initial lesson. Each framework has with it a suggested introductory lesson. These lessons are especially simple as far as curriculum content so that the concentration can be on how to use the framework. The teacher can choose any lesson as long as it meets this criterion. The important part is actually doing one together with your students rather than just explaining how to do it. As teachers, we may feel that our directions are explicit, but often our students do not hear or do not understand our meaning. Time spent modeling the process is useful for helping students achieve the specific end results, but it is also useful because it teaches students how to brainstorm, in a general sense, within any framework, whether working independently or in small groups.

Make the Frameworks Student-Owned

Frameworks that are partially filled in or even drawn and copied by the teacher often are too teacher-directed and become another series of "fill in the blank" worksheets for students. When students brainstorm and draw the parts of the framework as needed, the framework becomes student-owned. Students must express thoughts and concepts in their own words and are given feedback and clarification about the appropriateness of their thinking. Teachers are given insight into how students think and how they approach a problem. Brainstorming and writing give students the opportunity to place information into long-term memory. Students become active participants in their learning.

Eliminate the Paper Crunch

Encourage students to draw their own frameworks, to design a size or shape that is appropriate for them. An added benefit to the teacher comes when a paper crunch hits, as they so often do, and your supply of copy paper is limited. Early in the year, set aside the number of sheets you would have used for copying one of the frameworks; have your students draw this framework instead, saving those sheets for an activity during the paper crunch.

Using Time to Save It

By presenting so many different activities in all curriculum areas, your time spent in teaching and modeling any framework becomes doubly beneficial. The framework can be used today in math, next week in science, next month in reading, as well as in music, art, and physical education at any time. Once it is modeled, the teacher should still remind students of important points in its usage, but these instructions become briefer and briefer with each use. Knowledge of framework use is cumulative, so that students taught a framework in third grade will be able to use it with minimal modeling in fourth grade.

The Anecdotal Records

Included on page 231 is a sheet that can be copied. At the beginning of the year, make a notebook with a page for each student. Attach a sheet of blank self-adhesive address labels to a clipboard. As you are walking about the classroom during independent or group work, use these labels to jot down information about individual students. At the end of the day, place them into the notebook on appropriate student pages. This is a practical and time-saving way to keep very organized anecdotal records on each student.

We're Here For You

Feel free to contact us with any questions or suggestions. We'd love to hear from you. We're also available for workshops to model just how to make frameworks work in your classroom or to encourage their use throughout your district or school. Contact us through Libraries Unlimited/Teacher Ideas Press at the address below.

Libraries Unlimited/Teacher Ideas Press
P.O. Box 6633
Englewood, CO 80155-6633
(800) 237-6124
or
e-mail:
lu-editorial@lu.com

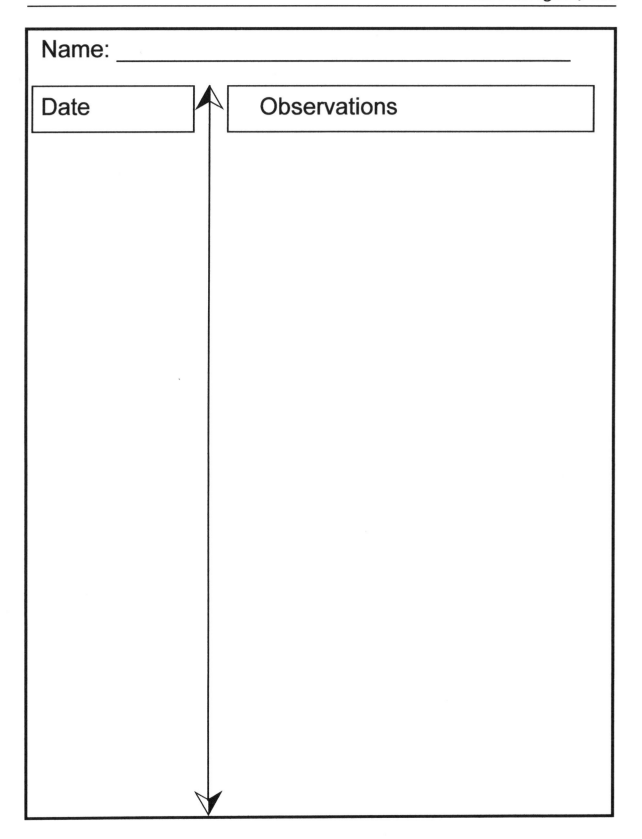

Name: _____

Date	Observations

References

Adams, Richard. *Watership Down*. New York: Avon, 1975.

Banks, Lynne Reid. *The Indian in the Cupboard*. New York: Doubleday, 1980.

Barrett, Judi. *Cloudy with a Chance of Meatballs*. New York: Atheneum, 1978.

Beyer, Barry K., Dr. *Eastern Hemisphere*. New York: Macmillan, 1990: 490–96.

Bishop, Claire H., and Kurt Weise. *The Five Chinese Brothers*. New York: Coward-McCann, 1938.

Buck, Pearl S. *The Big Wave*. New York: Aladdin Books, 1989.

Burchfield, Jean. *United States Presidents, Pictures to Color, Facts to Learn*. Washington, DC: Youth Publications/Saturday Evening Post, 1977.

Burnett, Frances Hodgson. *The Secret Garden*. Philadelphia: Lippincott, 1962.

Cherry, Lynne. *The Great Kapok Tree*. San Diego: Harcourt Brace Jovanovich, 1990.

Clifton, Lucille. *The Boy Who Didn't Believe in Spring*. New York: Dutton, 1973.

Dann, Calin. *The Animals of Farthing Wood*. New York: Heinemann, 1979.

dePaola, Tomie. *Strega Nona*. New York: Simon & Schuster, 1975.

Eaton, Deborah. *Move It!* New York: Simon & Schuster, 1992.

Elwell, Peter. *Cinderella*. Chicago: Contemporary Books, 1988.

Flack, Marjorie. *The Story About Ping*. New York: Viking Press, 1961.

Galdone, Paul. *The Gingerbread Boy*. New York: Seabury Press, 1975.

——. *The Three Billy Goats Gruff*. New York: Houghton Mifflin, 1987.

Littledale, Freya. *The Magic Fish*. New York: Scholastic Book Services, 1967.

Mahy, Margaret. *The Seven Chinese Brothers*. New York: Scholastic, 1990.

Mallinson, George C. *Science Horizons*. New Jersey: Silver Burdett Ginn, 1993.

Munsch, Robert. *The Paper Bag Princess*. Toronto: Annick Press, 1980.

——. *50 Below Zero*. Toronto: Annick Press, 1985.

——. *Moira's Birthday*. Toronto: Annick Press, 1987.

——. *Thomas' Snowsuit*. Toronto: Annick Press, 1985.

Myller, Rolf. *How Big Is a Foot?* New York: Atheneum, 1962.

——. *New Webster's Dictionary of the English Language.* New York: Consolidated Book Publishers, 1974.

Norton, Mary. *The Borrowers.* San Diego: Harcourt Brace Jovanovich, 1991.

O'Brien, Robert C. *The Secret of NIMH.* New York: Scholastic Book Services, 1982.

Ohanian, Susan. *Garbage Pizza, Patchwork Quilts, and Math Magic.* New York: W. H. Freeman, 1992.

Polacco, Patricia. *Pink and Say.* New York: Philomel Books, 1994.

Prager, Annabelle. *The Surprise Party.* Toronto: Random House of Canada Limited, 1977.

Pryor, Bonnie. *Mr. Munday and the Space Creatures.* New York: Simon & Schuster Books for Young Readers, 1989.

Sendak, Maurice. *Where the Wild Things Are.* New York: Harper and Row, 1963.

Scieszka, Jon. *The True Story of the Three Little Pigs.* New York: Dutton, 1989.

Siegel, Robert. *Whalesong.* Chicago: Crossway Books, 1981.

Sperry, Armstrong. *Call It Courage.* New York: Harper and Row, 1968.

Steig, William. *Roland the Minstrel Pig.* New York: HarperCollins, 1968.

Van Allsburg, Chris. *The Stranger.* Boston: Houghton Mifflin, 1986.

Wagner, Jenny. *The Bunyip of Berkeley's Creek.* New York: Bradbury Press, 1977.

White, E. B. *Charlotte's Web.* New York: Harper, 1952.

About the Authors

Patti Tarquin taught second and third grade in Canandaigua, New York for 14 years. She also was an adjunct professor at the Community College of the Finger Lakes. Upon leaving teaching she became an Educational Consultant in New York State. In addition to consulting, Patti is an itinerent Special Education teacher for the Special Children's Center in Cortland, NY. Patti, her husband Jim, and daughter Emily live in Cazenovia, NY.

Sharon Walker taught second and fifth grades in Blue Springs, Missouri for seven years. She moved to Rochester, NY and taught math and computer programming in the Palmyra-Macedon Schools for one year and math at Canandaigua Academy for six years. Upon leaving teaching, she was the New York science and math educational consultant for a textbook company. She is presently employed by Kideology as their educational coordinator, does independent consulting, and is on the review panel of a new math edition. Sharon and her husband Ed, Ontario, NY residents, are especially proud of their family, Shelly and Bill Talarico, Jeff Bratcher, Melissa Bratcher, Allen Walker, Tim Walker, Kim Jeffrey and their grandson Zachary Jeffrey.